HUSH
MA

BY MAMET

The sale of this book without its cover is unauthorized. If you purchased this book without a cover, you should be aware that it was reported to the author as unsold and destroyed. The author has not received payment for the sale of this stripped book.

This book is a work of non- fiction. Names, characters, places are products of the Author' s imagination or are used fictitiously. We as people can help change the world.

Copyright © 2007 by Mammeh Kamara Bangurah.

All rights reserved, including the right to reproduce this book or portions therefore in any form whatsoever. For more information, address Mamet books, PO Box 953. Pocono Summit, PA 18346.

ISBN: 978-0-615-16244-7

Manufactured in the United States of America.

For more information regarding special discounts for bulk purchases, please contact Mamet books at 1-866-511-0789.

ACKNOWLEDGEMENT

I would like to thank all the wonderful people that helped me achieve my dreams.

My dreams have been to help stop abuse. I decided to write this beautiful story of love, strength and courage of one girl. There are millions of Kumbas out there that would help change society, cultural and traditional abuses.

Thank you very much for purchasing this book. Because of this purchase, knowledge has been passed to help a little girl not to live in a world of abuse.

Special thanks to Mr. & Mrs. She-man of Colorado, for helping to educate me that in turn motivate me to help others. May God bless you and I hope to meet you someday, my guardian angels.

Mr. Edwin Kamara, thank you for helping to edit this book and giving me your wonderful words of encouragement. May God bless you and your family.

Mr. John and Paulette Shaw, thanks for your help in editing this book, for your warm welcoming my family and myself to the neighborhood and for your encouraging words. May God bless you and your family

INTRODUCTION

- Society is to blame for domestic violence, wife abuses and beatings. We as people can approach this by discouraging the widespread of abuse that is practiced in Islamic and non- Islamic societies.
- Most religions discourage polygamy marriages. To some society, it is traditional and believed that what makes a man, is to marry more than one wife. Men want to prove their superiority and abuse their sexual pleasures.
- Girls married off young is a local tribal and/or cultural tradition. Marriage should be established on mutual understanding, acceptance and approval not arranged. Its an ignorant belief to have families marrying off girls as young as 12 years old.
- Female circumcision also called female genital mutilation is also a societal and cultural practice. It is believed that when a woman is circumcised, she would stay faithful to her husband because she would

have no sexual feelings. Women have been mentally, emotionally and physically scared by these practices. Victims are at risk of contracting the HIV/AIDS virus and other sexually transmitted diseases during the process, because of the use of one instrument in multiple operations. There are 120 to 150 millions of women in the world that have been subjected to this practice and millions of girls are at risk of undergoing these ill practices. There are complications in the process like severe pain, shock, hemorrhage, urine retention and ulceration or the genital region and injury to adjacent tissue. Hemorrhages and infections can cause death. According to the WHO the consequences include damage to the urethra resulting in urinary incontinence, painful sexual intercourse, sexual dysfunction and difficulties in childbirth.

- EDUCATING SOCIETY OF ALL PRACTICES CAN STOP THE ABUSE. WE CAN HELP STOP SOCIETY ABUSES.

DEDICATION

This book is dedicated to:
The pillar of my life, my mother, Marie.
I thank you for putting us, your children first,
I love you and may God bless you.

My better - half big teddy bear,
my cubs' boo-boo, poochi-poo and mama belle.
Thank you for believing that you can do
anything you put your mind to. I love you.

And to women all around the world
that can relate to this story.
Stay strong and keep hope alive.

CHAPTER 1

"Go kumba, go, left, yes, yes, no, no, no, right, kumba, I say right".

Kumba could hear her mother's shrieking voice from the cheering crowd. I know she's there somewhere; smiling with her ivory teeth cleansed with salt, substitute for toothpaste. The air filled with red dust from Kumba and peers stomping around and into each other, scrambling to catch the scared chickens that seek a safe haven from the excited kids. It's Friday, the Holy day, a day to rest from their sweaty work schedule; they'll go to the Mosque later and pray. At the race, the drummers came from different tribes, their beat tell a story of their conquering forefathers; the wives take turns to express their love for their husbands by dancing exotically to their talent of different drum beats in front of them.

Strong smell of the proud fishermen is one of so many fragrances polluting the air. They've parked their pampa, which is the fishing boat made from logs of bamboo trees layered flat and attached together by rattan ropes; some can afford a motor and those who can't, make paddles from the logs to move around manually. Their wives who grow the cotton themselves weave their nets. A fisherman makes love to his favorite wife before heading to the sea. Luck from a wife brings prosperity to a fisherman and he'll make the catch of the day.

The past ten-moon announcer has always been Yabom Posseh the fairy; she's one of many wives of voodoo priest Pa Bai-koko. It's been rumored she's not human but a fairy that loves the human race and decided to join them on earth; with the help of her husband Pa Bai-koko who'd used the power of his voodoo herbs to try and recreate her to look human. Anatomically, he'd cut down the famous cotton tree in the village, used the branches to extend her height, the cotton to build her flesh but cannot find any herbs that will help improve her shrieking voice so she can communicate with others. Her husband claims he's the only one allowed to communicate with her, that's the way it should be to protect her fairy beauty. Yabom Posseh has never aged a day in her life nor has she gained weight or have stretch marks from all the children she'd been popping out every year. Sitting on her high chair crafted just for her, Yabom Posseh who's nursing her twins, the ninth and tenth of her children uses her voice to command the start of the race. She has both kids tied on her back, uses her naturally over built breasts to comfort them, which keeps the twins under control. Yabom Posseh throws her extended breasts over her shoulders to reach the twins to suck from her back.

Ninety percent of the women in the village have their breasts exposed, which makes them good mothers. They're always ready to feed their children, eighty percent of whom depend on their mothers' milk as source of nourishment; the remaining twenty percent they get from rice or corn pounded in a mortar and cooked as porridge. Early morning fresh milk from the cows with sugarcane water is blended into the cooked porridge to make a satisfying meal for the newborn. The adults also enjoy the porridge by adding limejuice to give it the zing taste for their taste buds.

Kumba's mind was focused on one thing, catching the chicken. Half naked first borns, tramping bare footed on the earthly soil they're familiar with. Their bare feet that wears shoes or slippers for holidays only, has grown so many keloids from the earthly chirped stones, broken bottles or unsafe remnants embedded into the dust. Red dust painted bodies screaming and scrambling all over each other wanting the same thing. Rhythms of the drums sound louder and exciting by the seconds. Chief Pa Sorie of the Temne tribe sat in his handcrafted chair made from the bark tree, his initials scribbled with gold dust mined from the local river and polished with elephant dung.

In his village of about fifteen hundred residents, Chief Pa Sorie as he was called is responsible for three hundred of the villagers, mainly consists of his four wives, sixteen children, mothers, mother in-laws, father in-laws, brothers, sisters, cousin, aunts and uncles. Naturally planted vegetables and fruits are their source for food. Men and grown boys hunts daily for animals in the forest to be brought back to their wives, who had already cut woods and gathers dry hays, which they inserts into three stones shaped like a triangle; uses kerosene fuel to lights up the fire and placed the big pot of water to cook the meat. At the end of each day, the smoked black bottom pot was scrubbed with sand and wood ashes; a local cleaning remedy that brings out the shiny silver color it had when purchased. It's a myth, that a clean pot makes you a good and clean wife; people would look forward to eat your food.

Rice grown on muddy soil, eaten daily as their staple food is harvested two to three times a year. The shelled rice when harvested is spread out on a sheet of cloth to be dried under the sun. The dried rice would be placed in a mortar and pounded. It's then transferred to a flat, round medium, rattan made plate called 'the fanner'.

The women shakes 'the fanner' left to right and gets the pounded rice in the middle. Gently tossing the rice in the air, a way to get rid of the pounded off dried shells, that flew over leaving the solid rice grain to fall back in 'the fanner'. When all the dried shells have flown off, the rice is washed and cooked. When there is shortage of rice, the villagers turn to their fresh vegetables of cassava and yam they've grown to be boiled and eaten with stew. The cassava leaves are also used to cook the best sauce that's been enjoyed for centuries. Pounded cassava leaves are cooked with palm oil derived from the palm tree, roasted peanut pounded and grinded with a bottle on a board to a creamy paste; Fish caught by the fishermen baked and added to the source with sea salt that gives the cassava sauce a succulent taste. Sometimes animals like squirrel, deer's or birds caught for the day are added to the sauce but would be given to the husband because wives believe their husbands should have the best. The best child of the day would get the remnants from their dad. The yam leaves are also cooked the same way, but thinly sliced instead of pounded.

In the small village of Maphyshon (ma-fee-sewn) every elderly male is called uncle; female aunty and all the children are cousins or sisters and brothers. It's difficult for a visitor to distinguish a real uncle from the others. Adults in the village work together to raise the children, they're all related because of the highly practiced polygamist life.

Each of his wives has one eye on Chief Pa Sorie and the other on their first-born. Uncircumcised boys, usually from birth to ten years old have their penis and foreskin dangling all over their nakedness. Circumcised boys from eleven to adult, have leaves stringed with ropes tied tightly around their waist preventing any exposure of their new manhood before marriage. Girls have cloth call the lappa covering their vaginas; covering their breasts is forbidden in their young age for fear a man will not be able to tell if they're ready for matrimonial duties. Both sex Scrambled and rolled in red dust with their half siblings to catch three chickens. Five first born, three chickens, two will loose, three are rewarded the head, neck and the chicken feet. It's a myth that when you eat a chicken head, you become wiser, the neck will make you stand above all others or be a great leader, the chicken feet will make you dance extraordinarily to the tune of the drums.

Chief Pa Sorie is respected by his villagers and looked up to as a wise man like his father Chief Pa Bai-loko before him who married his youngest wife at ninety nine years old, when she was only fifteen to make her his twelfth wife.

Kumba remembered vividly at an early age when everyone in the village was preparing to welcome the new bride and her family, who were escorting her to grandpa Chief Bai-loko's village. Hawa is her name; she was a gift to chief Bai-loko from her father from the neighboring village, Tutu. Hawa's father, Chief Foday was grateful to Chief bai-loko for rescuing his village at the time of drought. Since Chief Bai-loko inherited the chieftaincy from his father the great late Temne warrior Chief Bai-bureh Kamara, he had donated all left over harvesting to the Tutu village, which is one hundred miles away, because they have drought. It's been rumored that an old lady once passed through the village of Tutu on her way to the village of Seisi. The old lady was very thirsty, hungry and penniless; she stopped at Tutu and begged for food and water from the villagers, who in turn shooed and drove her outside the village where she died and her corpse left for the vultures to eat. There was another stranger passing by Tutu who witnessed the death of the old lady and tried to help her but was too late. The old lady last words were "tell the villagers of Tutu, that I have cast a spell on them, they deny me water, water will be denied to them, they deny me food, food will be denied to them". The villagers of Tutu ignored the old lady's spell and call her crazy. When the first drought hit them, they said it was just a coincidence. It's been a century already, the village of Tutu has had drought year after year, now some of the villagers do believe the myth, that there was once an old lady who cast a drought spell on the village because their ancestors had been greedy to share food and water with her. The Village of Tutu rivers run dry occasionally, villagers would have to walk fifty to seventy miles to get drinking water. If lucky, it rains three times a year, if not, only twice which makes harvesting limited. The villagers' source of getting fresh fruits and vegetables is from neighboring villages.

Kumba vividly remembered Hawa constantly wiping her tears through the transparent veil that was used to cover her face. After the wedding ritual that was performed by the high priest called the Imam, friends of the groom escorts him to the village center where they all sat around entertained by the local drummers and dancers as they drink an energy herbal potion until the bride arrives. Four old widows from the brides village will escort her, covered up to protect her skin that had been waxed with burnt palm oil and herbs, face cleansed with clay dug from the village running river, believed to give the bride a special glow on the wedding night.

At a younger age, Kumba never understood why Hawa was crying on her wedding night. She remembers when her dad married his third wife Mama Bayshay. Kumba was three years old; she could see Bayshay dancing and laughing to the beat of drums under the veil. Bayshay was active then, and crazier now. Kumba's mother mama Siah told her that Mama Bayshay's craziness is genetic. Children born after twins are named Bayshay, they're the black sheep of a family and usually a handful. Pa Sorie will beat his other wives only when they deserve it, but with Bayshay, they fight almost everyday, because she's stubborn as a mule, and takes no orders. Kumba could vividly remember the first time she witnessed a husband canning his wife. At age five, taught to carry a pale of water balanced on the head, Kumba decided to take the shortcut home. Balancing the pale of water on her head, she witnessed a humble wife lying faced on the floor as her husband used all his energy to cane her. Kumba flinched with every whip that landed on the woman's back leaving scars and sometimes dripping of blood. Kumba counted twelve strokes before the wife got up grabs the ready pale of water she'd set aside and headed to the washroom. Kumba walked off wandering what had provoked such punishment. In her household, her father often canes Mama Bayshay and Mama Hawa, but Mama Mariama and Mama Siah are exceptional cause they stay away from situations that'll annoy their husband. Kumba rushed home and told her mother of the beating. Growing up herself, Mama Siah has endured the abuse, she prayed and tries to be obedient to avoid it.

"Kumba my child, there are good wives and bad wives. Our husbands have great responsibilities and don't have the time to be patient with a bad wife so they cane them hoping they'll be good"

"I am always going to be good Mama, I don't like the beating" Kumba innocently promised her mother.

"Yes Kumba, you should always be good to your husband and pray everyday". Mama Siah taught her children the meaning of prayers.

"When you pray it's like talking to God and he'll help you," she once told Kumba.

"But Mama, I thought the Voodoo Priest is there to help in times of trouble"

"The Voodoo Priests are not God Kumba, they use black magic and tells you only if God answers that things would change. So you see child, that's why I try to pray to God myself and he's been helping me". Kumba tries to pray every night before going to bed. After witnessing the horrible scene, Kumba talk to God about it that night,

"God, I saw something bad today, a husband was canning his wife because she was bad. Please make me good, so when I grow up I'll be good to my husband. I thank you for this day God, for my Mothers', father, brothers and sisters and all living things, Amen.

The four widows dropped off Hawa at grandpa chief bai-loko's compound, they handed her over to the four other old widows in Maphyshon village. The drummers stay outside and entertain the adults, all the children are sent to bed when the moon is no longer visible. Kumba couldn't sleep with all the commotion going on, she got tired of tumbling and turning, decided to lay still on the straw bed she shares with her mother and siblings to enjoy the joyful beating of the drums. As the night goes by and the moon started to disappear into the clouds, rhythms of the drums changed to slower beats. In between the drums' pause, Kumba could hear Hawa sobbing loudly.

"Sobs of happiness and sorrow", Amy her half sister, best friend and three years her junior told her.

"Dah" Amy rolled her eyes, pretending to be smart, wriggling her tiny malnutrition frame, hands on her hips.

"They're happy because it's their wedding day, sad for leaving their mama and papa" Kumba couldn't quite analyze it, but she didn't push no more buttons. Amy is nick named chatterbox. Her lips never stay shut for long, she's a good free advocate, as young as she is, and no rumors in the village get past her.

" It's hereditary" Mama Siah said of Amy.

" She blabs just like her mother Bayshay". My mother can't stand Bayshay, worst of all, she has to share a husband with her. All the wives make sure nothing secretive is let out, or it goes back to their husband. Bayshay thought squealing on the others will make her Chief Pa Sorie's favorite, but she's the one that gets in trouble because she loves to stretch the truth. The other siblings can't understand how Kumba gets along with Amy. In reality, she hates her gut, Amy had tried several times to get her in trouble, but Kumba maneuvers the situation and let her fall into her own trap.

Amy and Kumba lost the chicken race. Kumba tried to be brave, went straight to the back yard where she had a pale of water to bathe. Amy mopes and cries openly, because she loves chewing the chicken foot, she hadn't got any over the past five Fridays.

Chief Pa Sorie loves his children; he tries not to differentiate one from the other. The children know that chief Pa Sorie pours love on them, but the mothers paint a different picture of Chief Pa Sorie's heart. Bayshay once accused Chief Pa Sorie of being a hypocrite to her children, because when he went to the city, he bought more clothes for Mama Siah's children than hers. Bayshay has no proof; she was devoured by curiosity and jealous. The other wives ignored her comments; they know for sure, Bayshay's always trying to deprave the children so they could turn on each other.

The chicken race always starts at six a.m and ends at seven a.m every Friday, which is considered Sabbath day in their religion. They are Muslims. At eight a.m, everyone of the scholars is showered, dressed in uniforms and sit on hand woven straw mat for breakfast, which consist of rice porridge made with tamarind juice, long grain cooked brown rice with fresh brewed palm oil. The flavor this morning is beanie, made from dried pounded sesame seeds. Some days, the rice is flavored by the caindah powder, which is derived from the lokus seed, a rare African fruit, that's in a pod similar to the green beans. Lokus fruit can be enjoyed differently, some like to stir it in water until the velvety mustard color juice thickens to be enjoyed. It also can be moistened with saliva and the velvety juice sucked. Like the sesame seed, the lokus is also pounded with dry fish, pepper and buillon to make it more appetizing and eaten with parboiled rice marinated by palm oil.

By eight forty five a.m, each of Chief Pa Sorie's children are seated in their hand made school chair and table crafted by the local carpenter to get an education. Their local calendar is the moon; it's counted yearly after an individual is born to tell their age. A child starts school when he or she has five moons. There's only one school in the village with three classrooms, two teachers who are bribed by Chief Pa Sorie to keep them in the village. Every now and then Chief Pa Sorie tries to recruit new teachers, but no one wants to work in a remote village, they prefer the city where there is excitement.

Teacher Sesay as he is called, is the senior teacher of the school. Teacher Momoh Sesay had just graduated from the famous Milton Margai teachers college in the city and was returning home to his village to share the news. He stopped by Maphyson to greet Kumbas' grandfather, Chief Bai-loko. Chief bai-loko was his fathers' first cousin. Teacher Sesay laid eyes on his second cousin Abie, Chief Bai-lokos' daughter by his fourth wife Salay. Chief Bai-loko knew Momoh Sesay couldn't afford to pay the dowry for his daughter so he traded his daughter for a teacher in the village. Teacher Sesays' father is a farmer with three wives and eighteen children; made up of fifteen boys and three girls. It was a curse on him, grandpa Chief Bai-loko once stated. Lots of boys are bad luck because they take away the family riches; girls bring riches to the family. To marry a girl, the dowry consists of three matured cows, five sheep and a dozen chickens for food preparation. In the calabash, which is a container made from the shell of a gourd, they put twenty-four karat gold jewelries, a hand woven straw praying mat, a thasbear which resembles the rosary that the Catholics use, sewing kit, a Quran, twelve yards of white lace, different mixture of nuts including red and white kola nuts. Two suitcases filled with clothes, perfume, slippers and lingerie. A new bride honeymoons for a month before she's thrown to the elder wives to assume her extra responsibilities. Depending on how many wives the husband already has, the wives usually rotate two to three nights in his room. They get passed over when it's their menstrual days or breast-feeding period.

The first or older wife gets to make all the rules in the household. The husband relies on the first wife to keep the other wives alert and meet his needs, even though some tend to be stubborn and malicious. In Chief Pa Sories' household, Mama Mariama is the eldest wife. Kumbas' mother; Mama Siah, came six years later into the marriage. It's been rumored that mama

Mariama is a witch. Being the first wife, and Chief Pa Sories' first cousin, Mama Mariama who was determine to further her education but was cut short because her parents, like all the rest, don't believe a girl should have an education.

"Girls with a lot of education don't want to get married, they feel superior to a man, and when they do get married, they want to wear the pants in the marriage" grandpa Chief Bai-loko once stated.

Since Kumba could remember, Mama Mariama, she's been in isolation; Mama Bayshay once stated that Mama Mariama coughs and vomits blood after coming from a witch scavenger, Mama Siah giggles at her remarks. Mama Siah knew that Bayshay does not care for Mama Mariama, which is hysterical, cause all they share is a husband and Bayshay rumors about Mama Mariama being a witch was just silly. Mama Mariama contracted Tuberculosis at the hospital when she went in to have an elective c-section. Her baby Salay was breeched and premature; she was given a fifty-fifty chance of surviving. Grandpa Bai-loko had summoned the voodoo priest to intervene and find out if it was the work of a witch that made her granddaughter breeched. Pa Bai –koko is highly respected in the village for his miracle work. He's the witch voodoo doctor; no one exactly knows how old he was. It's been rumored that he's walked on the soil for over two hundred moons. No one gets to see his face; his body is completely shrouded up to be protected from evil force stronger than him. When asked once about the voodoo priest fate, when he dies, if he does die, will he go to heaven or hell, grandpa Chief Bai-loko ingeniously replied.

"Neither". He stated that voodoo priest are in both worlds, they're good with their herbal remedies to cure impossible disease and also have the power to delete a human life. For every remedy of his work, there are so many charities to be done. Kumba and Amy once snucked around Pa Bai-koko's compound, their curiosity was correct. There was no room to breath; his entire animal shed was packed. Even though Pa Bai koko have five chicken coops, there was no space for them to walk. He has enough cows, sheep's, goats and ducks to feed three villages for couple of weeks. Pa Bai koko inherited the animals from different villages. After charities of goats, sheep's, cows or chickens are performed to thank the spirits and ask for help; the live animals are forbidden to eat, so they are donated to Pa Bai-koko. Fathers and mothers can't wait to donate their daughters as a gift to him. At present, it's rumored that Pa Bai-koko is managing a household of fifteen to twenty wives, this is excluding the forty to fifty children scurrying all over the villages. Amy once stated that she heard from Pa Bai-koko's daughter, who is her aunt and playmate, that one week of each month, his dad shares it with his invincible mermaid wife. The mermaid wife enters Pa Bai-koko's room through the roof and stays indoors for a week. No one including his wives or children sees Pa Bai-koko until the mermaid wife exits the room.

Kumba loves Fridays; they don't have to stay in school till five p.m. they're out at midday, hurry straight for their mothers' farms to mend it for them. The mothers go to the mosque for the Sabbath day prayers. At their parents farm, children are allowed to let loose; they sow vegetables and fruits, use the blacksmith made rake to get rid of weeds. Building a scarecrow is Kumba's favorite pass time; she gets to design it to her disliking and names it after her nemesis of the day. They take turn climbing trees to harvest ripe fruits to eat before the monkeys and birds get to them. Teenage boys leave the girls to start a fire as they wander off deep into the forest with their handmade bow and arrow to hunt for meat. While the girls boil vegetables, the boys will return with the catch of the day that can be a monkey, deer, rabbit, snake or squirrel for them to cook; excess meat is proudly carried home to show their achievements that they share with the rest of the family. After their hard work at the farms, boys and girls scatter around in different directions in the farm; they dig holes to pass feces, uses leaves to wipe themselves or rub off their butts on nearby trees. The feces are believed to be the natural fertilizer for the crops. They all meet at the local river where they do laundry, fetch water for the crops or to cook and drink and take a bath so that they don't go home dirty. Mama Siahs' farm is the richest in the village. She is the " bateh", meaning the favorite of Chief Pa Sorie and envy of her rivals.

CHAPTER 2

CHIEF PA SORIE CAME home for the summer vacation. He had just completed a year from Fourah Bay College. Being Chief Bai-loko's first born and first son, he'd exceeded the age of marriage, but he was an exception. Chief Bai-loko believes a man with an education is wiser, but Chief Pa Sorie's mother, Mama Mariama had other plans. Since her niece Mariama named after her, was born, Mama Mariama had helped her sister rear her to be a chief's wife. Mariama was only fourteen years old when Pa Sorie came for the summer break. His intention was to help in the farm, teach on days that teacher Sesay can't come, and to help his father sell kola nuts to the Gambians so that he can earn extra money before going back to college. It wasn't a surprise when approached on the topic of marriage. He knew it was coming, but not so soon, and because of culture and tradition, he couldn't refuse his parents request. It was very tough to find out who his bride was going to be, but who was he to object.

Mariama his first cousin had been like a sister to him all his life, now a wife for life, and no love, just a female to produce his heir for the chieftaincy throne. Mariama's school days were ended at age fourteen to be a bride and serve her husband. Mama Mariama was pregnant on her honeymoon and left with her aunt, namesake, now mother in-law while Pa Sorie went back to complete his education. In four years, Mama Mariama had three kids, Sorie jnr. Ishmael and Bintu before going on a strike. Its taboo to refuse your husband sexual needs. Mama Mariama had done that for a year without confiding in no one her personal reasons. For every time she refuse to perform her bedroom duties, she got beating by her husband and later by her mother in-law. Mama Mariama become depressed and attempted suicide twice. No one could get her to confide in them, why she behaved the way she did. Pa Bai-koko, the voodoo priest was called upon to intervene. Pa Bai-koko did not intimidate Mama Mariama. He labeled her as having four eyes. Two visible, two invisible that only light up when the sun sets to visualize objects beyond this world. Mama Mariama got tired of the beatings and decided to make known the secret she'd embedded for a year. 'Ignorance is next to madness'. Mama Mariama was angry at herself for waiting over a year, embarrassed to let her mother in-law know that her reason for living asexual, is because, she's trying to prevent herself from being pregnant. Mama Mariama was astir when her mother in-law promised to help by taking her to the neighboring village to meet with the family planning nurse who'll give her birth control pills.

After college, Pa Sorie decided to travel around other villages in search of gold and diamonds. He got the idea from his college roommate, who'd left a year before graduation to seek gold and diamonds. Keita was his name. Rumors had it, he now owns five houses in the city, married four wives back to back and had little rascals running all over his ten bedroom mansion compound. Keita no longer paid to work on peoples' mines for more gold and diamonds; he bought a mining land and hired workers. All he does is sit back with colleagues of his status, drinking attaya tea and collecting his accrued wealth.

Chief Pa Sorie was doing fine for the first year he spent in Kono. His journey was cut short when he was summoned to return home to his pregnant wife by his father Chief Pa Bai-loko. Mama Mariama was carrying her fourth child and very sick. The local doctor that visited her wasn't sure she'd survive the pregnancy. Pa Sorie hurried to be near Mama Mariama's bedside. With the help of herbal medicine, Mama Mariama made it past her first trimester.

Pa Sorie was off again, but this time not for business. He had met an eleventh grade student and fell in love for the very first time in his life. Her name was Siah and a citizen of Kono village. Siah was not born of Chieftaincy blood her parents were local farmers. Siah's father sometimes takes a side job at the mining pits.

Kumba could remember when she was three years old; Mama Siah had received a sad message from her mother, Mama Kadiatou that Siah's father had died. He was mining with fourteen other guys in a cave for diamond, when one of those unfortunate accidents happened. The cave collapsed, burying all living humans in it. Mama Siah was devastated, she's been squeezing left over grocery money and been waiting for two more moons before she can send whatever she'd saved to help her dad open up his own business. Mama Siah's father was forty-three years old; he left two wives and nine children. Mama Siah is the eldest of nine siblings. Siahs' mother is a Fulani from Conakry. Fulani's do not marry outside their race, but with Kadiatou, Siah's mother, it was an exception. Grandma Kadiatou's father, Pa Jallow, was best friend with Frank senior, Kadiatou's father in-law. Both dads, whom were business partners had made a pact to have their children wed, and they saw to it that it happened. Frank senior had also died tragically in a collapsed pit. A voodoo priest had once warned Frank jnr. to stay away from mining gold and diamonds; his star kept coming up negative on getting rich. Frank jnr. ignores the voodoo priest's prophecy, so he had decided to do mining as a side job and farming fulltime. Frank jnr ignored Kadiatou's plea, not to go into the mining caves. Since the death of Kumbas' maternal grandfather, Pa Frank jnr, grandma Kadiatou had been very miserable and stressed; because of culture, she was married off to her dead husband's younger brother. Kadiatou's child Siah was twenty and married; Kumba her sister, whom Siah named her first child after, was eighteen and Finda was sixteen. They were all married and gone. Pa Frank Jr's younger wives were shared to his brothers who married them; so were his younger children whom would be raised by the surviving brothers as theirs. Pa Sorie had great respect for his late father in-law Pa Frank jnr. Pa Frank jnr, one of the open minded African men; wanted her daughter Siah to attend college, but when Pa Sorie came to ask for his daughter's hand in marriage, he didn't object; instead, he gave Siah the opportunity to choose getting an education or getting married. Siah choose to be with the man she fell in love with; Pa Frank jnr. respected her decision and gave his blessings.

The love story started on a special day. Pa Sorie is sitting in the veranda of the one bedroom cement house he was renting. Everyone in the village of Kono has eyes on him; it's rare for a visitor in search of gold and diamond to rent a cement house. You must be rich to own or rent a cement house. Majority of the miners that travel to Kono to seek diamonds rent mud houses that are less expensive. On this nice beautiful evening, Siah was walking home with her friends from taking a private lesson in mathematics that was her weakness. Unnoticed by Pa Sorie, Siah chats away with her friends as she wiggles her size four frame down the road. Siah was aware of the effect her beauty has on men, but she'd managed to ignore all of the temptations and concentrate on her education. When her best friend Isatu dropped out of school in the tenth grade to get married, Siah vowed never to make such a stupid decision. At first Siah was angry with Isatu; but there was a rationale. The dowry paid for Isatu helped pay off her father's debt he'd accumulated over the years to start up a business that failed. Unable to pay his debt and facing disgrace with shame when sued to the Chief; who's also their local judge, he sold off his daughter to a husband fifty years his daughter's senior. Young and fragile, Isatu was thrown into farm work, not only hers but also to mend the farms of the elder wives who have aged. She'd named her first-born Siah after her best friend. At such a tender age, married and with a baby on the way, Siah had been there for her best friend. She'll go to Isatu's farm after school and help with the plowing or planting of vegetables and fruits. One day as they were working, Isatu went into labor, with no medical team around, Siah called out to the experienced old folks regarded as midwives for help. Siah was sent to build a fire and boil water for the birth. She did as was ordered and when she returned with the hot water, she witnessed the amazing birth of a new life. In the sun shaded hut waxed with elephant dung, a lady was sitting behind Isatu gently wiping the sweat from her forehead and temples; another lady was kneeling between her wide spread legs with a cloth instructing the shrieking and crying Isatu to push. Standing still with tears flowing down her face, Siah watched as the head the shape of a coconut covered with blood and slimy yellow foul smelling liquid makes it way out of Isatus' tiny body and into the waiting arms of the woman kneeling. One of the ladies who have been burning a small knife over the fire Siah had lit handed it over to the kneeling woman who used it to cut what looked like a long rope detaching the baby from the mother. Gently she wrapped the crying bundle of joy in the cloth, singing a joyful song as she hands the baby over to Siah. Siah was instructed to take the baby outside that is the culture; to introduce the new member to nature.

Siah is Daddy's princess; she gets her way around the house, which brought up animosity among her siblings and stepmothers. Afraid for her daughter's life, Kadiatou takes all her children to Conakry once a year to be cleansed by the voodoo priest against witches and evil spirits. Siah is a replica of her Mother; long wavy black hair that has to be cut once a month because it keeps growing beyond her buttocks; pointed nose, magical eyes that could hypnotize anyone, caramel tanned skin, mixture of daddy Frank jnr's dark color and Mama Kadiatou's pale epidermis inherited from her Fulani tribe.

It was love at first sight for Pa Sorie. With Siah, she refused to notice the dark, handsome young man and heir to the Chieftaincy of Mapyson. Rich, he's very rich was the rumor around the village; Siah could care less, she'd set her goal which is to pursue her Education to the end. Who can resist Pa Sorie, no one; he's got all the qualities a woman wants in a man, above all, he's well mannered. Rumors fly faster than the wind; young teenage girls dug into their pan boxes to get out what fairly good dress they could find. Rubbing their nappy hair with burnt palm oil and straightened it with a hot comb that leaves it shimmering in the day light. All dressed up, their mothers will give them freshly cooked rice with chicken or beef sauce to be delivered to the new stranger in town which is the custom. Mothers are not only feeding and being nice to the stranger, they're also hoping their daughters will be noticed and end up with a suitor. In Pa Sories' case, divorced, even widowed women his senior wanted to be noticed by him. It's scary but his father had prepared him well for the tempting world of different women who'll want him for his money or love. In his college days at Fourahbay College, Pa Sorie ignored all the beautiful girls that came his way, paid attention to his studies to have a good GPA and looked forward to going home every vacation to spend time with his new bride Mariama.

Mariama was very young and immature. Though well trained by her aunt, Pa Sories' mother and her name sake, how to be a Chief's wife, the teenager in her sometimes submerge which frightens her husband. Pa Sorie was encouraged by the elders to discipline Mariama; "you start by giving her six strokes with the belt, if she doesn't change, get a cane from the bush and increase the beating" they told him. It was hard on Pa Sorie to beat Mariama, but he had no choice or the villagers will think he's a weak man and being the heir to the Chieftaincy throne; they look up to him for guidance. Pa Sorie's father, Chief Bai-loko, will not accept any weakness from his boys. If Pa Sorie had defied him, he'll send him off to be punished by the elders and abdicate the throne to the stronger sibling.

No love; less communication and when they do communicate, he wants food or wants his water ready in the bucket for his bath. Arranged by their parents, Pa Sorie and Mariama's marriage was in turmoil. Sex is compulsory and a job that can be avoided only by menstruating or breastfeeding. A wife is punished when they refused to mate with their spouse. Some husbands object to birth control pills, they claim it's taboo, "why should healthy sperm be destroyed, the more children a man can produce, the richer he gets and proves to be a strong man" the elders reminds them. A man can marry as many wives according to his budget; his needs are always fulfilled. Each wife is given a farm, for every season and the wife that harvest the most crops will get the best gift. In a household, children are born every year and are allowed to breast-feed a year and a half to two depending on the husband. A wife is forbidden to sleep or make love with her husband when breast-feeding; that's why the husband has the other wives to fulfill his needs. A husband usually takes on the second wife when the first wife is having her first child. Cheating is considered a sin and forbidden. The in-laws will advise a husband to seek another wife promptly when a baby is born to give the new mother enough time to breast-feed and bond with her baby.

Pa Sorie was in no rush to get a second wife, he had made a promise to himself that his second wife will be someone he loves and finds for himself. His in-laws, aunts and uncles didn't have enough time to convince him to seek a second wife cause he was gone back to college when the first child was born. He returned in a year to wean the baby off breast milk and got Mariama pregnant again before returning to school. Mariama produce a child every year, it got her depressed and she became very insubordinate. ✺

CHAPTER 3

Siah was a challenge for Pa Sorie, he's used to having girls throw themselves all over him, but with Siah, it's like he never existed. She totally ignored him. Pa Sorie tried many times to have a conversation with Siah who never replied back, all she did was smile and walk by. Pa Sorie's integrity was insulted but he swallowed his pride and sought the advice of the village boys on how to start a courtship with one of their girls living there.

"To get a hard headed girl to like you, you should go around her friends and be financially generous to them, they'll bring her to you on a silver platter". The myth is true. Pa Sorie befriended Siah's friend Siaba, bribed her with jewelries, clothes then asked for her help to get Siah's attention.

"A friend in need, is a friend in deed", Siaba coaxed Siah into noticing Pa Sorie. It took a while but she gave in, and to her, it's like having another male friend. Pa Frank jnr, Siah's father had agreed to the wives plea for all the girls to have an education, but he also instructed them to make sure they kept their decency; strictly no sex until married. Girls are married off as young as eleven or twelve years old when they start developing breast. When the parent finds a spouse, the elders are notified. The village elders will come over, pick up the bride to be, take her away to be enrolled in a secret society away from their friends and family that knew them as kids. They'll escort her back after a month all dressed up with fancy clothes, jewelry, drummers leading the way on the streets, elders chanting the words "she's a woman now" behind and lead her to the waiting parents and groom to be. Siah now fifteen had been recognized as a woman since she was twelve. Most of her female siblings and friends that she went into the secret society together with to become women are now married, have two or three children. Siah intimidates men in their village.

"She's too proud and will never make a good wife" they stated when Siah turned them down for marriage. Mama Kadiatou sometimes gets stressed when one of Pa Frank's daughters from his other wives gets married; the rumors of her daughters no longer pure for marriage never stops. Girls are married off according to their moons. The higher the moon, the first to wed. Pa Sorie was not looking for a wife, but seeing Siah changed his mind. She glitters when the sun rises and glows when the sun sets. Any man will be insane not to make such a beauty his bride; virgin or no virgin, just her presence in a house will make a man the envy of his friends. Pa Sorie didn't want to believe the rumors in the village about Siah even though culture and society will not permit their future chief to marry a girl that's been deflowered so he decided to take his college roommate's advice,

"Why eat the whole cake when you can have a piece and be content". The first time Siah smiled at him was a day for celebration. Pa Sorie bought soda for every miner down at his site, overwhelmed with happiness. Siah was happy over the intriguing way he sent her expensive gifts, she sent him thank you letters and reminded him that their relationship should not go beyond being lovers cause she had no interest in marriage; Pa Sorie accepted her decision. In his college days, all the relationships he had were consented intimate ones, no strings attached, but with Siah he's confused. One day when they converse, she will pretend to be this innocent girl, another day, she'll chat all matured which drives Pa Sorie to move to the next level of their relationship. Their date has been going to the movies. Siah tries not to be seen a lot in public with Pa Sorie because of her parents' respect in the community. The courtship is a strain on Pa Sorie; slowly, he's falling in love with Siah, has to jab himself to wake up and smell the coffee cause she never returns the affection so he's sticking with the initial plan. Siah refused to give the rumor mongers the benefit; she let the rumor about her enter one ear and exit the other; since she had turned couple of the want-to-get married men down, she's been concentrating on her books and hoping that her Knight in shining Armour who's not in a rush to get married will come trotting by. And there he was, Pa Sorie. He was the only man that accepted her request and she was starting to like him a lot. Pa Sorie made sure that he takes Siah out once a week and days he can't see her, he'll send messages and gifts through Siaba. She was the first girl he'd dated for five months and hadn't been intimate with, he studied her and looked for the best way he can coax her petite body into his king-size waiting bed. Siah was very shy when he kissed her for the first time. Her soft black lip lines with moist pink lips are intriguing. Pa Sorie savored them, as she stood motionless and didn't indulge; it was getting very tedious for him. "Next Saturday will be the day," he decided. He can't control his testosterone any longer, her petite figure, round and firm butt cheeks, ejecting breast with pervious nipples kept taunting him. On Monday, he couldn't focus at work and left early to catch Siaba who'll deliver the date letter to Siah. Five days to go he counted; sleeping was the solution to make the day go by faster which made him miss her walking home from school on Monday and Tuesday. It's Wednesday, he'd missed her ivory white teeth smile; he needed to see her or he'll be forced to go and hide in the bushes behind their house and get a glimpse at her. Pa Sorie's wish came through, Siah came straddling down the red dusted road with her friends chatting and laughing; she smile at him but kept walking by. They've decided to keep the relationship discreet, fear of the promise she made to her father not to do anything stupid as long as she wants to be in school. Beside them, only her friend Siaba knew of their relationship, and she can be trusted, everyone else just speculated on the affair. Pa Sorie eagerly returned the smile with a peck and quick left eyewink; he'd held the memories of her last glance at him and retrieved to his bed hoping what just transpired between them would be repeated in his dream. He'd sent her the date letter with Siaba that was their discreet way of communicating.

It is the hamartan season; Siah wrapped her mother's old lappa around her tiny bare frame as she sweeps away dried leaves the cold hamartan wind blew off the trees. It's Saturday morning, Siah made sure the yard was well swept, pots washed, checked the barn to make sure there was enough firewood for cooking. Work well done, will prevent a second call to do it again. She like the other female siblings in the household helps their mother and stepmother's prepare breakfast, which consists of rice porridge with a loaf of bread and butter made from goat fat that their father treats them to once a week. On other days, leftovers from previous nights are warmed up or during harvest season when there's plenty, cassava or yams are served for breakfast. Pa Frank jnr's marrying the other wives was a big relief on household chores for Mama Kadiatou. Polygamy is accepted in their culture; her Christian teacher on a missionary work in their village had taught Siah it's a sin to marry more than one wife. At fifteen years old, Siah objects to her father's cruel intention towards her mother and stepmothers, she refused to endure her mother's enervation by giving into Pa Frank jnr's demands. Growing up, she hates to witness the physical abuse Mama Kadiatou went through; now a teenager, Siah made a promise to walk away from any marriage that involved physical abuse. Nenneh Kadiatou, meaning mother Kadiatou never complained; one day, Siah boldly asks her why she let papa Frank hit her like one of his children.

" I was bad Siah, and when you're bad, you get punished" she replied like a two- year old child giving a truthful answer. At fifteen years old, Siah now came to grips with reality that life never comes with syrup on a golden platter; one has to search for the syrup. Siah couldn't understand why majority of the men have to marry more than one wife; she could hear their Imam's words clearly when asked the question on polygamy, "our fore- fathers, fathers, brothers and sons should marry more than one wife, for example, our children need to be breast-fed, there is that time of the month you women go through menstruation between all of the drama in women lives, there's no time to spend with the husband" he paused.

"Men, I mean we are like dogs," he continues
"If you don't feed us, we tend to stray away and you know what the Quran says about that, it's a sin to commit adultery, so by marrying another woman, a man can avoid going to hell". When Siah narrate the imam's story to her teacher, she laughed but apologized that she wasn't laughing at Siah but at what the imam said.

"Take this as your homework" the teacher told them "think about it and write down who will go to hell, a cheater or a man that marries more than one wife". The next day, Siah was the only one that got a hundred on her homework. She wrote down, 'one; it's a sin to cheat and two; it's a sin to marry more than one wife, either way, you'll go to hell. To be saved, a man should marry one wife and be happy'. She's been teased as the teachers pet in class; Siah can't resist being smart in class.

CHAPTER 4

SIAH'S YOUNGER SISTER IS the third wife of a famous dressmaker in town. Pa Frank was happy to accept the dowry; he wasn't only getting a son in-law, but he was getting the family a dressmaker for free. Siah searched through the pan box she shared with her siblings for one of the Ramadan dresses designed by her brother in-law. Ramadan comes once a year, that's when they get new clothes to celebrate the fete that involves going to the local soccer stadium in the morning to join the rest of the town's Muslims, who'd been fasting thirty days, celebrate the end with the Imams in prayers, chanting Arabic songs, dancing to the dulcet beat of the local drums and later settling down to eat some of their rare foods. The cotton lace she'd worn the past year at the Ramadan fete is perfect but wrinkled from all the squeezing in the pan box. She went next door to borrow an iron; since theirs broke, Papa Frank hasn't remembered to buy one from the local goldsmith. Why should he; Papa Frank's bubu is starched and neatly pressed for his daily trips, the rest of the household have to worry about how to borrow an iron frequently. Fortunately, Siah didn't have to borrow coal; she gathered the remnants of the charcoal from the fire she'd made to prepare breakfast earlier. Papa Frank's younger wife, who'd been voted the best hair braider by the majority of the females in the compound, threaded her hair with rubber thread instead of cotton to give it a shimmering look the day before. Papa Frank had built two washrooms and two latrines; one he shared with his wives, the other for the children. Siah hates to use their latrine that is always left wet by her siblings. The local latrine is built by digging a five feet hole, which is covered by a wooden box. There's a round cut in the middle of the box, which allows one to sit, placed buttocks in the little cut and pass feces that'll descends into the five feet hole. Old newspapers, papers from old used books or water fetched from the well to fill up the cleansing kettle are used to clean up the residues.

Since Siah received Pa Sorie's date letter, her mind has not been at rest, she became clumsier at everything; voiding frequent feces, she mistakenly dropped the cleansing kettle used by her and peers to wash off the residue in the latrine. She spilled some of the boiling water intended to bathe on her lappa, the well bucket suddenly becomes heavier and almost drags her into the well and she has to let it go. While taking a bath, Siah reminisce of how her day had started so far; rinsing the suds off her slender figure, she tries to stay calm and refused to let Pa Sorie's letter weaken her. This letter is different from all the others he'd sent her. This letter is a map en route into his residence; their dates had been going to the local movie theatre or taking a stroll around the farm roads where there're scarcely intruders when the sun starts to set. Siah asked permission from her father to attend a movie with her girlfriend Siaba. Papa Frank trust Siah; she's been going to the movies and comes home safe, he knew she will not do anything stupid to jeopardize her mothers marriage cause the mothers are held liable for their daughters actions. Siah heard rumors from her friends about what men try to do when they're alone in the company of a female, it's not different from the story her mother laid in front of her when she refused to get married.

"You cannot allow any man to touch you if he's not your husband, if you bring shame to this family, your father will slaughter us" she deeply warned her. Nenneh Kadiatou wasn't born yesterday, she's knowledgeable of Pa Sorie courting her daughter and aware of how voracious matured and experienced men act when around an innocent girl. Once a month, Nenneh Kadiatou takes Siah and her sisters to one of the older ritual women in the village who'll check them. Siah hated the visits which include undressing from head to toe, lying on the cold floor polished with dung; legs widely spread and they're not let up until they shriek in pain from the egg protruding into their virgin canal. Siah couldn't understand what the incentive of touching her private part was, but it brings a smile to Mama Kadiatou's face when she groans in pain.

Siah rubs her slender figure with her favorite pomade made from burnt coconut oil, medicated herbs and a touch of fruit fragrance that meliorate the once awful smell to a succulent pomade. The strings on her favorite slippers press on the corn of her toes, which was unbearable so she wiggles when walking to keep the strings moving. Mama Kadiatou's jewelries were at her disposal. Siah made use of them, the simple set, beautiful but won't attract fans. Out of sight from her household peers, she reaches down her cleavage and remove the crumbled up letter she'd hidden in her brassier; unfolds the wrinkles to read the directions. It was a long walk but preferable than the short distance where she'll have to encounter curious family and friends who'll want to know her destination.

The back door was left ajar just like he'd instructed, Siah walks into the dim room that has a wooden bench and food on a table covered with a white sheet. Pa Sorie was nowhere; she stood motionless as the rhythm of her heart beats echoes in her ears, the air was filled with the scent of cassava leaves, fresh baked clay and palm oil aroma; Siah nervously rubs her sweaty palms together as she gazes around to make sure it's her final destination. Rays were coming from an ajar door in the living room.

"Is that you Siah?" the voice comes from the room. She recognizes it.

"Yes" she nervously answered.

"Have a seat, I'll be with you soon", he instructs her. Siah tight-legged scrunch at the end of the bench, sweaty palms clasp together as she waited impatiently for Pa Sorie who walks out wearing shorts and a ronko robe worn only by the high priest or a society initiated man.

"Hello pretty girl" he greets her revealing his ivory teeth smiling.

"Hello" she replies,

"I see you made it okay, I was afraid of you bumping into someone that'll recognize you" "so do I, but no one looked familiar", she paused and noticed he was barefoot

"Did I come early? Cause you're not ready yet".

"No you're not early; it's very cold and I ran out of my grease".

"I can see"

"Don't worry, Ali is on his way with a jar of my favorite grease" he sits next to her on the bench

"You don't mind spending the day indoors with me right?" he boldly asks her.

"You mean here?"

"Yes here".

"Just you and me?" she tries not to sound childish or nervous.

"Is there a problem, Siah?" he dug for the innocence in her

"Don't tell me you've never been alone in the company of a man before" he said, Siah couldn't understand his motive at first, then it comes to her, he'd been listening to the rumors around and believes them too or he won't be asking such foolish questions. She decides to play along to the lame reputation,

"Oh yes-s" she almost choked at her lie

"I've been in the company of different sex". His eyebrows went up

"Are you hungry?" he changed the subject.

"A little".

"It's almost lunch time, I figured you'll be hungry so I'd asked Mama Iye to send me over one order of cassava leaf and one order of fish stew, pick your choice". Mama Iye is Pa Sorie's neighbor who uses her home as a local restaurant; her stepson the village carpenter made her some chairs and tables for customers to sit and eat in her living room. Her daughter's help her prepare three to four different sauces a day with snacks for dinner. Her major clientele are the single men that work down at the mines.

"I'll have a taste from each" Siah can't resist passing either of mama Iyes' delicious sauce.

"Okay then, here's a bowl and spoon dig in". Siah felt really special; in their house, there are two silver spoons that belong to and are used only by her father. Everyone eats with his or her hand including her mother. She look at the spoon offered to her, it resembles her fathers, but there's a problem; Siah had never used one. She quickly washes her hand in the bowl of water and started to eat.

"Why don't you use the spoon, it'll help protect your hand from smelling of food so you won't draw any suspicion when you get home".

"Don't worry, I'll wash my hand with soap and for your info my friend, I grew up eating with my hand; those things, I mean the spoon is too fancy" she tries to hide the truth. "Give me your hand" he stretches out his.

"Why?" she shyly sighs off.

"Come on" he takes her hand and gently place the spoon in the eating position and slowly helps her scoop the food up into the mouth he's been aching to kiss for a whole week. Siah's a good student and learns fast; she took over after the fourth spoon-feeding. "You're not eating?"

"What, you think I'll let you enjoy all that delicious food alone dear" he went straight into her bowl and ate from her serving. Siah chews every grain of rice slowly hoping it'll be time to go home when she's finished. It is a relief when Ali knocks on the door, she has just finished eating. Pa Sorie shocks her by cleaning up the dishes which makes Siah believe the stories of men that are educated and had lived in big cities. They help out with household chores unlike the men in the village who have everything done for them. Men in the village believe their responsibilities are to provide food, marry lots of wives and have lots of kids. Women are to reproduce, cook, clean the house, do the laundry and tend to their husbands farms.

Siah can't be seen, her only choice of hiding in the one bedroom house is the bedroom; she makes her way into the room, leaves the door a little ajar and can hear their chat and laughter. Pa Sorie and Ali became friends since the first day they met at the mines. Because of his bad stammer, it takes Ali half of a minute to utter a word; the kids in the village make fun of him. Their conversation seems like it'll never end, Siah lay on the feather bed weak from a full stomach and takes a nap. She came to consciousness by the warm touch caressing her cheek. Siah's eyelids flew open, her instinct is correct, facing eye to eye with Pa Sorie makes the present situation nerve wrecking, "Hello there, I can't resist touching this beautiful Fulani face of yours" he spoke softly and continues to caress her cheek. Siah try to control her shaking tiny figure that's already coated with goose bumps when he kisses her neck.

"Are you cold, you're trembling" he pulls the sheet over them and positions her closer to his now naked broad hairy chest.

"Get up now!" her conscious mind alerts her,

"No, if you do, he'll think otherwise" the unconscious mind tells her to play along. "Never allow a boy or a man to be alone with you or touch you," her mother words echo over and over in her ears that left her weak and confused. Too late to get out of the tangle web; Pa Sorie is kissing her chipped lips. Trying to be brave and stubborn is a disease; Siah defied her mother and did exactly what she was warned to abstain from.

CHAPTER 5

Mama Kadiatous' instincts were correct; the ritual old lady confirms it, Siah had been deflowered; Pa Frank jnr. was notified immediately. Siah was tortured mercilessly until Pa Sorie's name was dragged out of her bleeding mouth. Pa Frank took his complaint to the village Chief that summoned Pa Sorie immediately. Pa Sorie didn't deny the allegations brought up on him; he agrees to pay the ransom for taking advantage of Siah's innocence and set a date which should be no longer than two weeks to make her his bride and avoid shame. Siah's dream of getting an education came to an end.

Siah was relieved to leave her village and start a new life in her husband's village of Maphyson. It was a long wait, everyone in her village got a piece of the gossip and her friends who ignored it got to believe when they saw Siahs' disfigured and weak face on her wedding day. At age sixteen, Siah became Pa Sorie's second wife with their first child on the way. She had a difficult time residing in Pa Sorie's village. Mothers of young single daughters were furious their future Chief married a girl from another village, she tried to ignore the jealous villagers but the trouble she should pay attention to was in her own household. Mama Mariama, Pa Sorie's older wife had not said more than ten words to Siah since she joined the family; she'd make it clear on her first day of arrival

"Keep in your corner, when you cook, make sure it's for your husband and you, I'll cook for my children and me" Mama Mariama warned her in front of Pa Sorie who tried hard to keep the peace. Mama Mariama made sure Siah did all the household chores. Cooking and doing laundry at the local river for her husband and in-laws. Coming from a polygamous family herself Siah is not new to her environment, Love got her there even though, looking back, she should have inquired about Pa Sorie's marital status. She'd gone with the impression he was a single man seeking rich minerals in their village. In her spare time, she makes it a habit of going to her father in-law Chief Pa Bai-Loko's compound and do chores for her mother in-law. Siah looks forward to the two nights she shares with her husband. The birth of Kumba was a joy to her life, it erased the misery of being alone, and finally, she has someone that will listen to her voice.

While breastfeeding Kumba, Pa Sorie takes on a third wife. Bayshay is the voodoo priest Pa Bai-kokos' daughter. She is a gift from her father to Pa Sorie that he couldn't turn down. Bayshay had made it clear when they were kids that she'll fight any husband of hers who dare beat her. At age twelve, Bayshay had her first confrontation at the village well, where they fetch water, with Pa Sorie who was then seventeen years old. Pa Sorie tried to get ahead of her; she pushed him hard enough to make him tumble into the deep cold water. Luckily for Pa Sorie, he quickly grabbed the well poles tight and used his knees to balance his weight; out of breath, Pa Sorie fought hard to gain his strength, used the back of his hand and slapped Bayshay who retaliated by jumping on him, fighting back as the crowd looked on. For disrespecting the future Chief, Bayshay was publicly punished by getting caned naked in front of Chief Pa Bai-loko who was to be her future father in-law. Pa Sorie had no choice but to accept Bayshay as his wife due to the respect between the parents, but his household had never been peaceful since she joined the family. Bayshay does not only disrespect Pa Sorie in the house, she also tries to get the children to hate each other and also claims her children were special because their grandfather is a big voodoo priest who'd anointed his grandchildren with voodoo oil to make the children wise and lucky in life. Bayshay is into everyone's business, her husband doesn't trust her and never discuss his business with her for fear she'll make it front-page news usually the next day. Bayshay makes it a habit of fighting with either the villagers or at home with the other wives or husband with whom she picks fights on her nights with him to avoid making love, which makes Pa Sorie no longer feel guilty over the years of forcing her into having sex.

It's taboo to curse someone a bastard; Bayshay has made the word bastard food in her mouth, for her children, husband and anyone that cross her path she'll curse. She's been sued to the local Chief who's her father in-law so many times for using obscene language on her friends and neighbors. Whenever Pa Sorie has to pay off a fine in court for Bayshay's wrong- doings, he takes away her allowance. Bayshay without allowance is like a dog without food; 'a hungry dog is an angry dog; it barks and bites even at its owner'. An impatience husband usually returns disobedient wives back to their family. In Bayshay's case, her father, the voodoo priest Pa Bai-koko's status over shadowed her behavior; he sees nothing wrong with his daughter. He claims Bayshay took after him but it's a shame she came out to be a female, he once told Chief Pa Bai-loko. When asked why can't he cure his daughter from acting like a lunatic, Pa Bai –koko once testified at a hearing for his daughter and publicly letting the jurors in on a decade old secret. He told them that his daughter Bayshay, is ruled by a bad genie that makes her act up the way she does. Pa Sorie doesn't think it should be an excuse for Bayshay's behavior. All the elders in the village don't come anymore to settle a fight or judge the argument between the couple; Pa Sorie got tired of his father Chief Pa Bai-loko sending him off without listening to his complaint and warned him not to return until he can properly discipline his wife like a man should. When he tries to seek advice from friends, they told him,

"Beat her mercilessly".

"Take away her allowance". He did that already.

"Let her tend to the majority of the farm work" it made him intrigued with his friends' ideas. Bayshay is impervious and don't care how many punishments he imposed on her; she never change. In the seven days of the week, she'll have six fights but holds off on Fridays that is a holy day; she has to go to the mosque for Juma prayers. Bayshay's twin children Isha and Isa took after her; they've been brewing trouble all over the village since the day they started to walk. Pa Sorie learned to accept the fritter days and fact that he's been doomed forever for having Bayshay as a wife.

Hawa, Pa Sorie's fourth wife joins the family not by her choice. She was initially a gift to Pa Sorie's Father and Kumba's grandfather the late great Chief Pa Bai-loko who had eleven wives;

Hawa was to be his junior wife. Kumba had eaves-dropped on her fathers' conversation one day and heard him tell his friends that Chief Pa Bai-loko should have thought twice before taking on Hawa as his twelfth wife. "Hawa's too young for my ailing father" he puts it. Kumba used to know her as grandma Hawa, now she's Mama Hawa. It's a myth to marry an odd number of wives. Everyone knew Pa Bai-loko will eventually takes on a twelfth wife to have an even number of wives, but no one expected a much younger teenager from the village Tutu for a wife at his age. Grandma Mariama, Chief Pa Bai-lokos' first wife, had suggested he marries one of the widows of their faithful farmer Lasana, who'd died tragically of pneumonia. The widow Fatou is an experienced woman that needs no supervision and it'll be less work for Grandma Mariama who's responsible as the older wife to teach the new wife all the household chores. All of Chief Bai-loko's wives were startled when he accepted Hawa, a teenager, to be his wife at his age of ninety-nine. There is rumor around the village that Hawa had bad luck; it's her fault Pa Bai-loko never made it to see one hundred. The voodoo priest Pa Bai-koko had predicted, Hawa was Chief Pa Bai-koko's death warrant. Chief Pa Bai-loko turned a deaf ear to the warnings and went along with his friends' advice "the younger the wife, the better". Men in the village believes a younger wife make them look macho to their friends and they live longer. The myth was wrong this time. Chief Pa Bai-loko spent a week honeymooning with his new bride Hawa that is tradition for the newly married couple regardless of how many other wives the groom has. The regular routine of spending two nights with each wife will halt and resume after the honeymoon. Hawa had the last of him or what was left; Chief Pa Bai-loko was found dead on the last day of his honeymoon. Kumba never saw her favorite grandpa again since the night of the wedding festival when he had on his ronko gown which he loves because it was woven by his grandmother, Kumba's great, great grandmother Sento, the greatest cotton weaver that ever lived.

CHAPTER 6

Kumba had heard stories from her father of great, great grandmother Sento. "She was a woman of peace," he told them. Great, great, grandmother Sento traveled around different villages exchanging cottons for kola nuts. Her Ronko's were special because they were woven from cotton grown by many tribes. Every tribe knows the history of great, great, grandmother Sento and her famous ronko cloth that brought together the minds of elders and helped stopped tribal wars. She never sold her ronkos, she donates or exchanges them but she was rich from all the gifts that were sent to her from tribal Chiefs for her generosity. Great, great, grandmother Sento owned a piece of land in all the different villages and she made sure each of her children, grand children and great grand kids inherit a piece when they're born. Her legacy makes tribes afraid to fight each other over silly disputes because she'd warned them that they'd only be fighting their sweats. They're all farmers, each ronko had a piece of cotton from the farmers farm; she prophesied the punishment of fighting ones' sweat is bringing bad luck to the community. Chief's ronkos have ritual ornaments weaved in them, a woman still menstruating and under the age of fifty is forbidden to touch a Chief's ronko cause myth has it, they'll be barren for life. A barren wife is considered the maid of the family and a curse to her husband. Chiefs wear the ronko on their wedding day or when officiating at a wedding, to funerals and when in the local courtroom but it's immediately removed with the aide of his personal assistance who chants ritual songs while they put the ronko away in the pan box stashed under the bed in the Chief's private room. Only the Chiefs and their aides who are males from a higher society rank enter the private room. An aide has to go through all the twelve or so rituals to be able to walk into the sanctuary where the doors are always locked to prevent wives and children from intruding. It's been proven by the Elders that nosy wives were known to be barren or die and nosy children go blind and dumb to prevent them from blabbing what they witness in the Chief's private room. When a Chief dies, no one is allowed to see his corpse, instead the Elders that had initiated the torture of crowning him to the Chieftaincy are summoned immediately to the abandoned corpse. All witnesses that saw the corpse are taken away for a week to be cleansed ritually by herbs to erase their memory of how the corpse looked. It's rumored that the corpse of a Chief is taken into a secret hiding place in the forest where it's preserved with herbs for forty days. The embalmed corpse is mounted on a hook inserted through the abdomen with head down to drain every ounce of blood from it. The blood is collected, mixed with medicated herbs for special healing purpose. Kumba was told that the head of the deceased Chief will be cut off and preserved at an unknown site; the Elders bury the headless body when the villagers are asleep. The families are taken to the burial site forty days after the death of a Chief. The wives are kept in deep mourning and will graduate after forty days; their future lies with the Eldest son who inherits the Chieftaincy crown. The son takes in the youngest wife in three months or after being examined by the Elders to make sure she wasn't pregnant before taking her position as his concubine. The brothers of the deceased Chief are given the second choice of taking on their deceased brothers widow for a wife. One of the widows is forbidden to remarry; she's been regarded as the first lady and mother to the new chief. The first lady will live with the new heir to guide him into his fathers footsteps and make sure the work is done like the former Chief, his father would have had it done.

Being the youngest wife of the late Chief Pa Bai-loko, Hawa was taken in by Pa Sorie as his concubine. The Elders kept her until when she menstruates for three months, that was their proof that Hawa wasn't carrying the child of the deceased chief. When she joined the family; Mama Hawa immediately conceived her first child. Mama Siah and Mama Hawa had become friends before sharing the same man. Mama Siah couldn't stand the idea of Hawa being a concubine, nor to have a baby as a bastard, she personally pleaded with her husband the new Chief Pa Sorie to marry Hawa and make her child legal. It's illegal to marry your concubine, but Chief Pa Sorie can't say no to Siah, he loves her too much to deny her anything even though Mama Mariama his older wife was strongly against Hawa being a legal wife; Chief Pa Sorie defies her pleas and pleased the love of his life. Mama Hawa has been very grateful to Mama Siah and named her first born a girl Siah to express her appreciation. Baby Siah is beautiful as her namesake; she took to Mama Siah immediately. When guests visit Chief Pa Sorie's household, they usually mistake Mama Siah for baby Siah's biological mother because the baby is always on her back secured with a kente cloth.

Bayshay couldn't stand Mama Siah; she tried several times to anger her and start a fight. Mama Siah got tired of sitting down with the Elders to lodge her complain on Bayshay. Chief Pa Sorie had told her several times to be patient; he'll personally see to Bayshay but nothing's been done to control Mama Bayshay's bad temper. Mama Hawa was tired of the beating Mama Bayshay gives her and is ready to walk out of the marriage. One day, Mama Siah came from the farm just in time to catch Mama Hawa leaving with her bundle of clothes tied up in kente cloth, carried over her shoulder. "Where are you going?" Mama Siah asks her and notice her children were nowhere around.

"I am going to my village, I can't take this abuse any more Mama Siah" she burst out crying.

"Where are the kids?" she grabs the bundle from her hand.

"In the house, I can't take them, they're not mine".

"Of course they're yours, don't you ever say that", Mama Siah warns her of her motherly duties.

"They are his children, he won't come after me if he has his children" tears flow down her cheeks.

"Hush with that nonsense of yours, now you're starting to sound like that fool, Bayshay. Pa Sorie loves us all the same Hawa you know that, come on, I've got to put a stop to Bayshay" Mama Siah grabbed Hawa's hand and dragged her towards the kitchen. Bayshay was preparing dinner when she felt someone pull her hair and she fell backwards, Hawa grabbed Bayshay's feet while Mama Siah punched her face mercilessly until blood flowed from her nose and mouth. They tied up her hands and feet then used the cane to beat her twelve strokes each. When they finally released her from the bondage, she got her children and left. Bayshay filed a lawsuit with another chief; she believes her husband won't give her a fair day in his court. To her disappointment, Mama Siah and Hawa were only fined two bushels of rice, which Chief Pa Sorie helped his wives to pay. Since then, Bayshay never laid a hand on Hawa again.

Mama Mariama was in her own world; she rarely speaks to anyone except her husband. Being called the black sheep of the family does not move her, she chooses not to co-mingle with the other wives but she does not keep her kids from interacting with the other children' like Bayshay does.

Teacher Momoh tries not to give his students homework everyday. After they've helped their parents at their farms, they are worn out and do not have enough energy to go home and do homework. Teacher Momoh usually schedules all class exams on Fridays and bunch of homework on weekends to be turned in on Mondays. The only school in the village has up to class seven. The nearest high school is in the neighboring village that is eight miles away. Boys whose parents can afford it financially buy them a bicycle to commute to school, and for those that can't; they walk or hitchhike on the back of travelers' mopeds. Girls are forbidden to proceed to high school; they're married off as young as twelve years old and the groom can be from fourteen to one hundred years old. Most of the girls are spoken for since the day they're born or conceived. A friend of the new mother, a friend of the new father or a relative can pay a pre-dowry for the new baby girl as a promise to the parents she'll be a bride for their son when she comes of age. The betrothal parents will help the girls' parents financially to raise her. In return when the little girl is of age and can comprehend, she'll be introduce to her betrothal. Boys that don't have the means to further their education works fulltime on their parents farms harvesting fruits and vegetables to be sold at the local market and when they have enough money saved up; they'll commute to the city and sell their products wholesale in the big markets. They save up money to buy their own farm and prepare to take on a wife to help them. To the villagers, going to the city is like a path way to heaven. Every villager wishes to go to the city they've heard stories about, the cement and board colorful big houses, unlike the straw and mud huts in the village. In the city, there are machine driven cars of different models and colors and plenty of foods that you buy with money.

Chief Pa Sorie seldom shares his city experiences with his family. Kumba and her siblings get their information from travelers passing by or teacher Momoh who grew up in the city. Her father's friend son Sheku who was away attending college in the city spoke for Kumba. Kumba is in sixth grade and can read; Sheku who's nine years her senior sends letter through the bus driver to her once a month. The three years Sheku's been gone, he'd visited three times; he claims school was hard and studying to be a Medical Doctor is no joke. In one of his letters, he'd indicated that the reason he doesn't visit was financial problems; he has taken up a job at the local hospital working as an aide to buy some of his books. It's forbidden to communicate in depth with your future husband but greetings are allowed through the in-laws. The bus driver was aware of it; Kumba knows his arrival time and makes it a duty of secretly meeting him to pickup the letter Sheku sent and drop off hers. Kumba likes Sheku but not to be his bride at a young age; with all the stories she'd heard of the city, her dream is to further her high school and college education there one day. How will she convince her father? Mama Siah will be no problem, she'd been day dreaming of having one of her children further their education in the city; a chance she never had. But unfortunately, Kumba is her oldest and a girl. Girls are married off after junior high school, but Mama Siah was determined to set the record; Chief Pa Sorie will have to make an exception. Sheku spoils her, he sends her beautiful clothes and shoes that he buys with the money left after he purchases his books. Some of Kumba friends hang around her because she dresses nice; some can't stand her and are jealous because they are wearing left over clothes from their mothers, siblings or friends. Kumba will soon turn twelve and finish junior high; her fate is hanging on a thin rope, after the junior high graduation, Sheku can show up when she finishes her ritual to become a woman and marry her or she can convince Mama Siah to convince her father into letting her go to the city and live with relatives to further her education. At present in the village of Maphyson, all mothers of eleven and twelve year old daughters are having private meetings with the Elders of the women society that takes place every year at the same moon or month. By the end of the meetings, all the older daughters of each household are sent off with the elders who'd keep them out of sight for a month and initiate them into a society that'll transform them into women before going off into marriage.

Kumba knew her time was up; she'd graduated first in her class which was no surprise to her mother Mama Siah who was torn between respecting culture or paying attention to her daughter's plea for help by convincing Chief Pa Sorie to send Kumba in the city to further her Education. Afraid that her smart daughter will end up like her, Mama Siah decides to make the attempt and convince her husband. She had got one advice from her younger sister who was married off at age twelve.

"Siah, the best time to have your husband listen is when you're alone with him in the bedroom", she'd reminded her and swear on it. Mama Siah pulls out the nightgown Chief Pa Sorie had bought her as one of her wedding gifts. She has a drop of perfume left and she carefully hides it away from the reach of her children, especially Kumba who wears it to school. She's been saving it for special occasions. Chief Pa Sorie had been away at meetings with the neighboring Chiefs to share ideas of how they can better serve their citizens. It's Mama Siah's night with her husband; she took a fruit bath and prepared one for her husband. She was summoned just as she prepares to don herself, everyone in the village knows of the love Chief Pa Sorie has for Mama Siah; he openly shows it even though he knew it's hurting the other wives feelings, but to him, there's no way he could be a hypocrite and hide how he feels. Mama Siah always likes to be with him in the washroom when he's taking a bath, but tonight, she has another agenda; he'll just have to finish up by himself. Mama Siah joins him at the washroom, briskly rubs his back covered with thousand of keloids obtained from the tribal cuts he got when initiated into the Chieftaincy with hay and black soap. There are so many rumors of what an ordinary man submits to for the Chieftaincy title; the keloids on his entire back were proof of the many dagger cuts he received during his initiation process. He lost three toenails when he walked through the charcoal fire that's one of the many rituals. The Chieftaincy society is similar to the Poro society that is a step lower; they share the same rules but different duties, some of the rules are:

"No hissing at an initiated man, or your stomach will inflate and burst, no starring in their eyes you'll go blind, no cursing at them you'll be deaf and dumb".

To keep the society men on their toes, they held a meeting of the minds once a week in the forest to decide the fate of a bad witch. There're witches in all the tribes and many households, they are the ignorant vampires that go around hunting for human blood at night to quench their thirst. Many households have voodoo ornaments prepared by a voodoo priest to protect their families from mindless, jealous and greedy witches who prey on unprotected homes for innocent children to feast on. In Chief Pa Sorie's household they have sanctified brooms made by the voodoo priest hung behind the doors to prevent witches and special beads are weaved with thread and tied around the children's waist for extra protection. The poor villagers who can't afford to pay a voodoo priest for their protection became victim for the witch who invades their house and sometimes gets away with murder. A witch travels at night in the shell of a peanut as their airplane to get to their destination in seconds and returns back in time before sunrise. There have been several occasions when a witch is caught naked at sunrise by the villagers. Their stories had all been the same.

"We ran out of gas and couldn't get home on time" they'll testify in the local court where they're judged by the Chief after having publicly beaten by the villagers. If found guilty of the crime they commit, the punishment is death by fire, stoned to death or they'll be handed to the villagers who'll mercilessly beat or hang them to death. The Chief pardons some witches if the crime is not serious.

When Kumba was born, Mama Siah was told that her baby has four eyes. Two visible, two not. The two invisible ones that can't be seen by the naked ordinary eyes are said to be located at the nape of Kumba's head, which the voodoo priest said could be used to see through walls and witches. For the protection and safety of a child with four eyes, the parent usually consults a witch doctor to erase the invincible eyes for fear of a child making eye contact with a witch who is merciless. Mama Siah never used to believe witches can hurt their own immediate families until it happened in hers. When she was five years old, she got to know the old man lying under the tree in a hammock as grandpa; he was blind and always chewing alligator pepper kola nuts. At age twelve, Mama Siah's first cousin, Finda confessed to taking their grandpa's eyesight when she was three years old. When asked what was her motive to commit such a crime by the witch doctor, the twelve- year old told them she was mad because her grandpa never shared his nuts with her.

"Do you know what kind of nuts your grandpa was chewing?" the witch doctor asked her.

"No sir" Finda nervously replied.

"Here, this is the nut; it's called alligator pepper kola nut, go ahead take a bite" Finda chewed up the nut and almost choked to death,

"Here, you want more?"

"No sir" she cried out.

"You took your grandpa's eyesight for not sharing his alligator pepper kola nut with you, now you know the reason, they taste horrible and are not meant for children to eat".

"I am sorry grandpa" Finda cried out and ran off into the forest, the witch doctor restrained everyone from following her. Finda never returned. Couple of days later after the villagers have waited impatiently for her return; the witch doctor predicted the bad news. Finda, the sweet cousin with an innocent face will not be coming again to join her family, she had ran off with the group of witches to locate homes in other villages that are free of voodoo ornaments to seek blood.

CHAPTER 7

"Where are you going?" Chief Pa Sorie grab her hand when Mama Siah tries to dash out of the washroom.

"I am finished scrubbing your back"

"I didn't say you can leave, sit, keep me company," he orders her.

"I can't today".

"Why not?" he asks and slowly turned around revealing his bare wet body facing her dropped chin and eyes protruding twice the size of its sockets. "I—I –em-m-m" she stammers lost for words.

"What's the matter?" his eyes caught her starring in astonishment.

"What's the matter Siah?" she quickly turns away.

"Are you shy, it's the same one you've seen

many times" he reminds her.

"I have something to do".

"What is it that can't wait?"

"The clothes, I just remember—yes the clothes, I did the laundry, I need to get them in the house".

"Why is that? You can do it later or get the children to pick them up".

"No, some are delicate and should be taken off the grass carefully or they'll be ruined with all them dry weeds stuck on them", Mama Siah searches for the right excuse to exit. "It's not an emergency Siah, I need to talk to you".

"Can we talk later?"

"Why are you being stubborn today?" she sensed an anger building up,

"I am sorry if I sound defying, it just that I heard earlier it's going to rain this evening" she lied.

"That's strange, my moon reader didn't mention rain in court today". Their local meteorologist whom they call their moon reader predicts the forecast of the weather daily in the local court.

"He must not remember or forgets to announce the weather," Siah continues.

"Forget the rain then, what's really bothering you Siah, this is unlike you" he walks closer; she can feel his breath on her face.

"Come on spill it out or I'll spill this bucket of water on you"

"I already took a bath" she took a step backward hoping he won't carry out his threat. "Oh I know, but if I get you wet, maybe I'll be able to keep you in here with me" he smiles revealing his dark brown teeth covered with kola nut stain.

"I'll stay" Mama Siah quickly answers fear of getting wet.

"Well, well, are you going to tell me what's really eating you inside?" he finished scrubbing his feet and looked up at her beautiful face that hasn't aged a day since he married her. His other wives had gained weight since they had his babies, but Siah is the same size two or four he guessed and wrinkle free. Chief Pa Sorie makes sure he buys vitamins in the city and distribute them to each member of his family every morning so he knows Siah cannot be malnourished, she's just small structured.

"Are you going to talk?"

"You go first" she bows her head hoping he'll talk first, because what she has to say can't wait.

"Come on Siah, you know I'm very open". It's the custom; the wife never speaks ahead of her husband.

"I guess yours is important, that's why I said you can go first" she took the guilt off him. "It is important Siah, I don't know how you'll react," he sounds like he's about to bear sad news.

"I can take it, tell me; who died?" she squeezed her wet palms together waiting anxiously.

"You look sallow, are you okay?" Pa Sorie

reaches for her hand; she tries to control her shaking little frame.

"What's bothering you my love?" he asks softly and diverted his full attention to her.

"I'm just waiting to hear what you have to say" "it's not that bad Siah, look at you turning pale on me, trust me, I don't want to be the bearer of bad news, I have the Elders to do that" Siah try to calm her nerves.

"I was going to talk to you about our daughter Kumba".

"I know, you don't have to remind me, I'm already discussing with the Elders to have her in the womanhood society group this year, God knows it's about time she go through the ritual, come back and get ready to be a bride". Siah hypocritically puts it like she meant it.

'That's why I want to talk to you, Kumba can't go with her peers into the womanhood society this year" he let it out.

"But she's already the age". She acted confuse but wanted to hear more.

"I know, but I have other plans for her". Siah's dream was unraveling in front of her, but it wasn't a dream; he's keeping his promise to her.

"Please God, let me be right," she chants to herself, as she stood motionless and waited for him to continue.

"Remember my promise to you Siah?"

"What are you talking about?" she pretends not to remember.

"I have plans for Kumba; I can see she has all your traits, smart, motivated and lots of potential in life, you know I believe in education and it does matter to me if a girl is educated. In the college I attended, most of the students were girls, it's about time I start changing the rules in the village; a girl can further her education if she so desires".

"What about the Elders?"

"I haven't thought about them yet; I owe you this Siah, because of me you couldn't finish your education like you wanted to".

"It's okay, I have no regrets being married to you," she reminds him for the millionth time. Their secret affair that came out to be known made them rush into a marriage to stop the disgrace that both families were facing. Siah had to stop her schooling and become the second wife of Chief Pa Sorie, even though she loves him dearly, deep down if she was to go back in time, she wouldn't have taken that stupid route. To ease the pain of cutting her education short, Chief Pa Sorie had promised her that when they do have a baby, boy or girl, he'll make sure their baby continues were Siah left off, to fulfill her dream.

"Kumba will be going to live with my brother Sheik Abass in the city to further her education", uncontrollable tears flow down her cheeks, out of words; she fell into his naked body and cried helplessly.

"Thank you, thank you" she cried out.

"For what Siah? She's just like you but I took that opportunity from you. I won't deprive our Kumba of achieving her goal, not even if she fell in love down the road". As a bachelors degree holder himself, Chief Pa Sorie is against the traditional rules that girls shouldn't further their education. But his status as the Chief and respect by his villagers, presented him from voicing out his feelings. His father and forefathers ahead had all gone with the idea that a woman's place is honoring her husband, cooking, cleaning, producing lots of children and mending the farms. Chief Pa Sorie is aware of the consequences he'll face because of the drastic step he's about to take. He's the Chief, it'll all be gossip behind his back, no one will dare confront him as to what his reason will be for sending his daughter to the city. Kumba is the eldest and a daughter to Siah; his oldest son Sorie jnr. born to Mama Mariama, the first wife, will inherit the Chieftaincy and is being reared by the family elders for his future duties.

The news came as a shock to Kumba who's been having nightmares of what she'll face in the womanhood society and her wedding night. She's heard so many rumors from her peers of what transpires on wedding nights, the stories of the big anaconda with two or three heads that swallows and spit you out to give the bride a special glow; she came up with her own assumptions that brides are tied up and beaten mercilessly that's why they cry on their wedding night. The decision of her trip coming from her father was more puzzling because lately, Sheku's parents had been back and forth to meet with her parents. Kumba had thought they were there to organize her wedding; unfortunately, Chief Pa Sorie has summoned them to renegotiate her daughter's future. Mama Siah had the longest mother and daughter talk with her, which is the first time she'd been open. Her openness went as far as letting Kumba know that she shouldn't let no male figure touch her there; she pointed to the private part between her legs. Mama Siah made it known that it's okay to have a conversation with the opposite sex, but no touching until after the womanhood society and get married. Confused by her advice, Kumba didn't ask her reason on the touching subject but listens when her mother elaborates on her hygiene and appearance; especially the changes her tiny body will be going through and what to expect, but it's all normal she puts it.

Mama Siah gave her the traveling bag she'd got as a wedding gift from her mother Neneh Kadiatou. Kumba couldn't take all her beautiful clothes; her siblings grabbed most of them and convinced her she'll have prettier clothes in the city. There were no dry eyes in their household on the day of her departure. To the amazement of the villagers, Mama Mariama was crying, she doesn't like Chief Pa Sorie's wives, but their children are exceptions. Through arguments,

fights and malice, Mama Mariama will have her room filled with all of Chief Pa Sorie's children where she'll wrestle, sing and dance with them.
❇

CHAPTER 8

Couple of hours on the road to the city didn't impress Kumba; the stale scent in the air made her nauseous and forced her to swallow all the vomit saliva. Mama Siah had once told her,

"If you're nauseous, just smell your armpit or suck a lime" Kumba didn't favor the armpit thing, but at this point, she had no choice, there was no lime around. In the clustered van, she felt squeezed like she was in a can of sardine that made it very uncomfortable to take a nap during the long drive. Her stomach rumbled, it was hard to take a bite of the cassava bread that was packed for the trip due to the galloping of the van so she forced herself to fall asleep to get over the hunger.

"'Kumba, Kumba, we're here, wake up" the words rang in her ears like music. Kumba made sure she wasn't in dreamland. Slowly, she opened one pupil at a time and viola; her father was hanging over smiling down at her.

"We're in the city?" she manage to ask looking around the empty van wandering how long she had slept and lucky her father was accompanying her or no one would've noticed her. Kumba stumbled over remnants as she makes her way out the van to join her father. They had left Maphyson about noon; its mid afternoon sunny and humid, she was taken aback by the view in front of her; she'd never seen so many pretty colors, everyone was fully clothed, some girls have on shoes that match their clothes and bags with faces painted different colors that made them prettier. Hair silky, let down loose or tied up in ponytails. Some had long braids neatly done. Looking around, she did not notice anyone carrying a bucket of water on his or her head. Mothers carried their babies tied tightly on their back like the women in the village; deep yellow jewelries hanging on their necks and ears, some even have on the white shiny jewelries. Kumba found it strange to walk on the black tarred streets with her new shoes; it's her first pair. In the village everyone wears plastic slippers and when they have a feast, the local shoemaker will make them slippers using the skin of the cow, sheep or goat that had been slaughtered for the feast. The shoes she has on were a gift from Sheku a year ago and she'd never worn them, afraid the red dusty gravel in the village roads will mess them up. Their huts are waxed with dung to suppress the dust flying around. For the eleven years Kumba has been in the village; she had no idea other cars existed and in different colors and models, she's used to seeing only the van that makes it's trip to her village. Many cars, buses, vans and trucks pass them by; her eyes were all over while hanging onto her fathers gown trotting along. Her feet were sore and whatever little clothes she had in her handbag were weighing her little body down. Kumba's stomach rumbles as they pass the roast beef stand, the scent of freshly burnt meat mixed with peanut butter, onions and herbs fills her nostrils, she gulps down saliva that gathers in her mouth but it just made the situation worst. Her throat is dry and she aches for a drink, which make her cough few times. Chief Pa Sorie took her into a small shop that was filled with fresh food, candies, gums and drinks, he bought two bottles of drinks, opened them and handed her one. She hesitates, fear of not knowing what to do and watches Chief Pa Sorie gulp down the contents and she copied his action, which makes her choke and cough on the first gulp because it is a big one. It is the best water she'd ever drink; it is sweet and has a nice flavor with bubbles that tingle her tongue. Kumba took her time to savor the drink as she rotates it during breaks to read the label that reads "Fanta soft drink "and beneath it are tiny writings she couldn't make out. Her father gave some coins to the man in the shop for the soft drinks and they exit the store. She turns around trying to catch the name of the place her father got the drinks; she's sure looking forward to pay a visit there in the future and get more soft drinks. Kumba feels like she's in another world; the stories she'd heard of the city were not exaggerated, from the cement or board houses covered with aluminum roofs, some are rusted because they were built long ago. The beautiful color cars blinded her sight. In the village, the hay used to cover their mud houses are changed every year after the rainy season. Kumba almost got lost from her father because anytime she sees a tall building, she has to stop and look up to count the floors which makes her neck tired but she can't resist the scene before her eyes. When they got to the long line at the end of the road, she was very exhausted. The soft drink helped with her thirst but the hunger was another thing; her stomach is rumbling loudly for food. The smell of roast beef still lingers in the air that makes her current situation worse; but she won't dare disturb her father for food, she's a big girl and will be expected to hold whatever is bothering her until they get to their destination. They boarded the big and long bus called the 'poda poda'. There must have been one hundred seats all occupied. A gentleman who recognizes Chief Pa Sorie offers his seat to him. After the long walk that left her drenching with sweat,

Kumba was happy when her father offered to carry her on his lap where she got relief from her aching feet but the stale air in the poda poda did not help her hunger which turned to nausea. She held the drink in her for energy or the situation will get worse and will make her vomit and pass out from hunger.

Kumba's favorite snack is kola nuts. Mama Siah was astonished by how Kumba will chew the bitter kola nuts like the elders and enjoy it. She's aware that the bitter kola nuts help cure some stomach disease, but she can't endure the brown and orange stain it leaves on the teeth. As a concerned mother, she'd taught Kumba how to take care of her hygiene and warned her to stop chewing kola nuts.

"A beautiful smile will bring good Angels around you," she once told Kumba. Kumba reaches for her head tie and unties the edge where she'd neatly knot half a kola nut smuggled without the knowledge of Mama Siah, and quickly puts it in her mouth. It's a myth that old warriors chew on kola nuts only when they go to war and can stay for weeks in the forest without being hungry. The bitter, irony taste brings great comfort to Kumba. She doesn't like to swallow the residue so she slowly chews it over and over to get every last taste. The city is beautiful, but the people are not as friendly like the villagers. Kumba greeted the pedestrians; the older ones smile back, the younger generation just rolled their eyes, hissed or pretend she was invisible. Kumba noticed big beautiful cars pass by with women sitting at the back alone wearing fancy boubou, their heads wrapped up with what looked like two yards of material. Some have the material hanging down their back with a white, gold or silver box shaped crown securing it on the head. Kumba fell in love with the city, but she just can't bear the foul smell in the air. There were big gutters on both sides of the roads that takes wastewater into the little rivers where some people go to wash their clothes. In the village, water is precious not to be wasted; without water, the crops will suffer, that's why when weeks pass by and no rain, the well waters are drawn to substitute. What a difference, in the village, Kumba will have to go with a bucket to fetch water for drinking compared to the silver iron rod that pump out water with the twist of a knob; the water even tastes different. "This is the market place," Chief Pa Sorie pointed.

"Even though it's crowded, I use it as a shortcut to your uncle's house", he concluded. The tiny pathways are filled with mud, people everywhere, scent of different foods, raw, smoked and cooked. Girls carrying pales in their hands chanting

"Cold water, ice cold water five cents a cup, buy cold water and quench your thirst away" Kumba couldn't believe what she was hearing, water is been sold; the difference is, it's ice cold, compared to the hot faucet heated water that she just gulped down. She tags along and tries to catch up with her father, whose pace doubles through the crowd. Chief Pa Sorie stops a couple blocks away from the market place in front of a red painted house. The paint was peeling off and the wooden windows are cracked. There was a store in front filled with rice, sugar or even gari made from cassava. There is a woman about six feet tall, almost three hundred pounds dressed in a blue festival boubou; face filled with beige makeup that makes her dark skin look pale. Blue eye shadow to match her gown and brown eye pencil line was visible in between her black eyebrows; she has on blood red lipstick that smears on her teeth when she smiles. It looks like she also rubs some of the lipstick on her cheeks, cause they glitter with red and makes her look like a doll her father had bought her on one of his trips from the city when she was five years old. Kumba had stashed it away where no one could find it because the doll has so many colors on its face and it scares her siblings and her. The woman couldn't get up from the chair she was squashed in to kneel and greet Chief Pa Sorie, which is the tradition; instead, she bows her head to greet him.

"Kumba, say hello to your aunty Josephine" Chief Pa Sorie introduced her.

"Good day aunty" Kumba shyly said.

"How are you my child, come here, look how big you've grown, just yesterday I cuddled you at your naming ceremony; now you're even fit for marriage".

"Not until she's finished with school, Josephine" Chief Pa Sorie firmly puts in.

"Yes, after school, come on child, go to the back, your other aunts are there, your uncle will be home soon". Sheik Abass is Chief Pa Sorie's younger brother by the same mother. Grandma Mariama calls him the prodigal son, cause after schooling in the city, Sheik Abass declined his fathers' wishes to return back to the village and help in the family farming business. It was rumored that a woman cast a spell on him. That woman is aunty Josephine.

"She's from the Mende tribe, they're well known to use voodoo to keep their men", Mama Bayshay once told them, "they are known to do weird things to keep their men, example; they cook dry feces to feed them or even give them their menstrual water to drink by adding fruits to it so the men won't notice the smell" she will tell her friends who drool in wonder listening to what might be a lie or not. "Their little evil remedy works cause their men will never leave," she concluded. Mama Bayshay can be called everything bad, but this time, she might be right. Kumba hasn't seen his uncle since she was six years old. When he came from visiting the Holy Land of Mecca where he was initiated as one of the high ranked Muslims, and given the title of " Sheik", meaning the disciple of an Imam and can one day become an Imam himself; Sheik Abass called some of the Imams in the neighboring villages to escort him and help ask for his fathers forgiveness. Kumba could remember that day vividly; grandma Mariama cried uncontrollably at the feet of her husband to beg for her son's crazy behavior. Grandpa Chief Bai-Loko agreed to forgive his son because of the respect he has for the Imams that accompanied him. For Sheik Abass to be one of the family members again he should marry a girl from the village, his cousin Fatima, Mama Mariamas' half sister was given to him for a bride. Aunty Fatima was thirteen years old when uncle Sheik Abass married and brought her to the city. The six to seven years Aunty Fatima had been away, Kumba heard many rumors about her from Mama Bayshay. Couple of months after Aunty Fatima's departure, Mama Bayshay told almost everyone in the village that she got a message from a long distance cousin of hers that resides in the city that she had come across Fatima, and she looks like a skeleton. Mama Mariama lapsed into a deeper depression when she heard the rumors Mama Bayshay's been spreading around; no one could tell whether Mama Bayshay was lying or not. Mama Mariama swallowed her pride and begged Chief Pa Sorie to pay a visit to Sheik Abass's house in the city and check on her little sister. A month later, Chief Pa Sorie came back with the news everyone's been anxious to hear,

"Mama Fatima looks like bones with no meat

on" Chief Pa Sorie told Mama Mariama,

" But she wasn't being maltreated, it's due to her present situation", everyone looked around trying to guess what situation Aunty Fatima was facing. "Fatima is in child bearing way" Mama Mariama's face lit up with a smile, she jumped up and chants a thankful note for the bearer of good news. Some of her friends joined in the chant, and they danced to the good news all the way to her parents' house to pass on the news. Mama Bayshay can't stand good news; she rolled her eyes and disappeared into her room in shame. Five children later in six years, Aunty Fatima was pregnant again when Kumba met her. She was dressed in a fancy cotton clothes at home, which makes Kumba think she was going out, but she was wrong. Aunty Fatima wears only the best cotton clothes at home that other wives have the privilege to get once a year as a gift from their spouse. Aunty Josephine isn't blessed with children and Kumba also heard the rumors of why she was barren,

"She used to be a koro girl". To the locals, a girl is labeled "Koro" when they are sexually active with lots of men, use obscene languages, very loud and defy their parents. Rumors had it that she had terminated lots of pregnancies for different boyfriends and was lucky Uncle Sheik Abass picked her up to be his wife because she was a rich businesswoman. The locals believe she had used voodoo to capture his love, but

God had punished her by taking away the one thing a woman craves for in life, "A Child". Aunty Josephine was unhappy until Aunty Fatima came into the marriage and started producing a child every year. Uncle Sheik Abass's household had since been filled with joyful noises of children, but Aunty Josephine was not jealous, she embraced Aunty Fatima like her younger sister and spoiled the children who took to her immediately cause she spoils them rotten. In return, the children call her Mama and call their biological mother Aunty Fatima or "FA" by her first two initials. Aunty Fatima is different from her sister Mama Mariama; she's more open and chats a lot. Uncle Sheik Abass takes long trips to Cairo, he is in charge of helping men and women who want to visit Mecca, the Holy Land, but can't afford the trip, be able to do so. Uncle Sheik Abass meets with mogul Arabians who donate money to Muslims in under privileged countries in Africa as help for transportation to make it to the Holy Land.

CHAPTER 9

The Imam at the Mosque was mad at Uncle Sheik Abass for allowing Kumba to attend a Catholic High School. It was Aunty Josephine's choice. Uncle Sheik Abass had left the package to enroll Kumba in the Muslim school he'd helped build, but Aunty Josephine waited until he traveled, then took Kumba over to St. Joseph's Convent High School, where she'd attended and enrolled her. On their way to the principal's office, she narrates the importance of being a conventonian and the benefits it offers in life. She points out that girls that attend St. Joseph's Convent School are smart, get to attend the best colleges and always have the chance to be awarded scholarships to further their education in London and the United States. Aunty Josephine wasn't fortunate to further her Education, but got lucky to succeed in business that made her one of the richest women in the city and she married a respected man. High School is not only fun for Kumba, but she gets to learn lots of civilized culture from her classmates. Strictly, English is the language spoken in school; anyone caught speaking the tribal or local Creole dialect will pay a fine and be punished. Even though she wears uniform to school, Aunty Josephine bought her a box filled with fancy clothes and six pairs of different colors of shoes from the famous Bata shoe store. Aunty Josephine is excited having a well-mannered teenager at home, she also spoils her rotten. Kumba enjoys every part of it, but the best was what Aunty Josephine had done to her hair. She used to hate her nappy, coarse, tangled roots and will braid it and keep it on for months to avoid combing the nappy painful hair. She was taken to the salon as a treat from Aunty Josephine where the hairdresser permed and curls up her nappy length silky hair and bought a pack of colorful hair bands that make her look forward to combing and styling her shiny hair everyday. She also got tips on how to apply colors to her face the right way and later found out its called 'makeup'. Kumba like the changes in her life, she was happy her father made a good decision of allowing her to finish up her Education in the city. Thanks to Aunty Josephine and Aunty Fatima, she was quickly filled in on how to catch up on civilization.

When a baby girl is born, their ears are pierced ninety days later with a sewing needle threaded with black thread. The needle is used to guide the thread into the newly bored hole; half an inch of the thread is left with knots at both ends to prevent it from falling off. The thread is pulled back and forth from knot to knot every morning until the ears heal up. Twenty-two or twenty four-karat gold earrings will replace the thread after thirty days. Kumba noticed not every girl in the city wears the twenty-two karate " moraw-moraw" earrings as they were called. She was hesitant at first to take hers off and try the big fancy earrings that everyone had on, but her Aunts wears them, so she copied the present fashion.

Mama Siah was in dismay to see her little girl that left their village change in a year. Kumba couldn't wait for the school break to see her parents and siblings, but they all looked at her like another stranger passing through.

"It's me Kumba, it's me Kumba", she held out her hands smiling. Kumba was shocked by their reaction towards her; Mama Siah wrapped her tiny frame around her that makes her remember the story she'd learned at bible study class, "the prodigal son", and she felt like the prodigal daughter. Kumba spent a month of her summer vacation in the village, where she gets to teach her female siblings about life in the city and convince them it's her, but with a little flaw or upgraded fashion; and returned to the city for the rest of the vacation to take some math classes that was her weakest subject.

Back in the city, Kumba's friend, Juliet, asked her to escort her to Fourahbay College one day after their math lesson. Juliet is a Creole and a Christian; it's very seldom for a pure Creole Christian girl or boy to co-mingle with a country and a Muslim girl. The Muslims claim the Creoles are proud, educated and try to dominate them; the Creoles on the other hand believe the Muslims belong in the village where they can grow crops, not the city and they have no rights to an education. Kumba and Juliet only hang out at school but not in their homes afraid of "the not welcome sign" they'll receive at each other's house. Kumba caught up with Juliet at the bus stop and find out they don't have enough fare, so they hitchhiked all the way up the mountain road to the college. "What exactly are we doing up here, do you know this is a college and we're high school students?" she curiously asks Juliet.

"Remember the boy I told you about?"

"Which one, you have to be specific cause you've told me about so many"

"Oh please, this one is not like the others" she rolls her eyes, hands on her hips and sways left to right as she talks.

"This is the one he's in college"

"Yeah, well thanks for filling me in last, but don't you think he's your senior" Kumba asks the million dollar question.

"What's the big deal, in four years I'll be in college, it's not like I'm a kindergarten kid".
"Who else knows about this?"

"No one Kumba and I'm trusting you with this".

"Well you know me better Juliet, that's why you confide in me" she reminds her.

"Of course Kumba, I do trust you, but listen, he's a sweetheart and makes me feel special, but I'm scared to death" she confessed. Kumba was confused, she couldn't put it together; Juliet had dated high school boys, but never scared, why is this troubling her, "how long you've been seeing each other?" Kumba pried deeper for answers.

"Oh come on Kumba, you know I don't hide nothing from you. I met Desmond last week at the all high school sports; he was one of the judges that interviewed me for the hundred meter race". Juliet made it second in the race and had trained so hard. The record holder attends Annie Walsh High School that is their competition when it comes to the best education in the city.

"You know it's against the rules to date the judge Juliet, our rivals will put you on a spotlight". She stopped, turned to face Kumba.

"Kumba, I am so confused, there's something about Desmond that I like. On the other hand, my athletic career and scholarship are on the line", "Juliet, you need to keep running or you'll loose your scholarship". Juliet's' parents are counting on the scholarship funds to help pay for her education which will be one less burden out of nine siblings.

"Are you sure you want to meet this Desmond guy, look, there's a pay phone over there, you can call him and gently break up the date", Kumba can read from Juliet's facial expression that it was the wrong words she wanted to hear.

"I can't chicken out now, he'll think I'm immature especially when I've given him my word that I'll be there, that's why I brought you with me—God help me Kumba, I am so scared". She held Juliet's sweaty hands and rubs them gently.

"Let's go face the music then, it's just like any date you've had, the only difference is that he's a college student".

"Yeah I know, I'm so stupid Kumba, why on earth did I agree to meet with him?"

" Well remember now, curiosity killed the cat, I can't say you're making a mistake, it might just turn out fine".

"What if it doesn't?"

"Well, we'll never know unless we get there, come on let's go meet Mr. College man". Juliet smiled and held on tight to Kumba's hand as they walk the rest of the mile to the campus.

Desmond was everything a girl looks for in a boyfriend; he's six feet three inches compared to Juliet's' five feet two tiny figure. He's about one hundred and eighty pounds dark brown chocolate skin, red sun tanned hair with pearly teeth to compliment his smile. Desmond wasn't mad at Juliet for dragging Kumba along on their date; he's a comedian and jokes about it and makes them feel welcome

"Your friend is very shy" Desmond looks over at Kumba that laughs at his jokes but says nothing.

"She's not used to escorting friends to a dates," Juliet said giggling.

"You should meet my roommate, he's just like you, not a city boy and he hasn't dated any girls since he got here".

"Isn't that strange?" Juliet asks puzzled.

"At first when I tried to set him up with a date, he didn't show up, it made me think he was a-a-ahh" he waves his hand left to right.

"What, you mean he's gay?" Juliet said the word out loud.

"Don't say that word, he's not", " and how do you reach that conclusion?"

"Well, when he didn't showed up for the date, I confronted him because I was so embarrassed to face the girl and have no excuse for his behavior. But to cut a long story short, he confessed there is a beautiful girl back in the village waiting for his return after graduation to marry".

"Oh, he's a faithful one".

"Yeah, but that stinks, he's twenty years old, with all these beautiful girls on campus, whose going to board a bus to tell his betrothed of what little fun he's having in college?" Desmond smokes his remaining cigarette, puts out the butt and gulps down more of his beer. He'd offered

Kumba one, but she declined and got a soda instead, Juliet accepted the beer and drink with him, which was a shock to Kumba. Desmond finished his beer, got up, grabbed Juliet's hand and pulled her towards an open door.

"Kumba, I'll be right back" she scrambled behind him.

"There's a movie in the VCR, we'll be right back", Desmond sounds off and locks the door behind them. There is only one thing a male and a female could be doing behind a locked door, she learned it in biology class. Juliet surprised her. Kumba would never have guessed that she was sexually active, not with the innocent face she carried around school and her friends. Kumba turned on the television and watched the local news instead; the entrance door opened, she turns around but could only see the back of a tall dark guy closing the door. She'd never met Desmonds roommate, this might be him or a burglar, but he has a key, so he can't be a thief; she braced herself tight and prayed to be right it's the roommate or Juliet and Desmond will have company cause she'll break down the door and run in there for protection.

"Hello, you must be Juliet", the voice calls from behind. It's so familiar that she couldn't wait any longer but turn around to face it. Speechless, they both gazed into each other's eyes steadily in shock for few seconds.

"Kumba?"

"Sheku?" they called out each other's name as they ran over living space furniture with hands opened wide into each other. Sheku embraced her very tight; she could hear the blood pumping into his veins and heart beating to a sweet music. Kumba laid her head on his broad shoulder and was glad it was a familiar face.

"What are you doing here?" he loosens the hug but held tightly to her sweaty palms,

"I am escorting my friend Juliet to visit her boyfriend",

"Ahh-ah-ah, stop, it hurts" Kumba could hear Juliet crying in the locked room. Sheku stared at the door and quickly turned back to her.

"Is he beating her?" she innocently asks.

"Come lets get out of here, she's fine" he grabbed her sweaty hand tight and quickly pulled her out of the apartment. Once outside of the heated stuffy apartment, he heads straight into the woods, out of sight. Kumba kept silent and followed his path, Sheku pull up some lemongrass leaves and lays them under an orange tree and guides her carefully onto the freshly layered lemongrass without letting go of her hands and sat in front of her so close it makes her heart pounds faster. He smells of palm oil and pine, looks very different. It's been almost two years since they saw each other, but even when they did, it wasn't this close; he'll visit her father's house with his brother and stayed away from her. Sheku will give whatever gift he had for her to

Mama Mariama, cause she's the older wife and it's respect she delivers the gift to Mama Siah for Kumba. Sheku is taller and more masculine now.

"You've grown and more prettier". "I'm a big girl now Sheku, and I just turned fourteen, she boldly adds.

"I can see that" he looked at her, smiling provokingly.

"Do you know how long I've searched for you?"

"But why, didn't your parents inform you of my departure to come and further my education in the city?"

" Of course, but not in depth cause you know they were not thrilled by your father's decision. Aminata has been visiting your house to try and get more information about your whereabouts for me". Aminata is his favorite baby sister.

"I got a letter from her last week informing me that you're attending St. Josephs' High School. I was planning to come down next week and look for you after my final exams", he moved closer, which left her trembling. It's the first time in her teenage life she has been so close to the opposite sex. All her friends are dating boys already or married; but she'd promised her mother not to do anything-stupid cause she's been told about the incident of a boy holding her hands.

"Kumba, you're trembling, are you cold?" he quickly took off his shirt and put it around her shoulders and pulls her closer to his body. Sheku's big hands were holding her tight as she trembled out of control; he slowly caressed his neatly shaved cheek on her face. Kumba didn't know what to do; run or act matured and sit still. She closed her eyes and talk to God silently,

"God, please help me, I've never felt this way before, help me God cause this feeling is strange and I am confused".

"Do you feel warm now?" he asked. Kumba nod her head cause she didn't know how the words would come out of her trembling mouth. He pulled back to face her,

"Kumba, can I please kiss you?" she didn't know what to do, never been kissed before, she nodded her head again and closed her eyes. His lips met hers and she felt his tongue swimming in hers while looking deep in her eyes.

"Are you still shy?" he asks up close smiling, and rubbing her shoulders. It's in her mouth; it has a very strange feeling. In a second, her body temperature went from ninety eight point six to one hundred and one point; goose bumps all over her body, heart beat racing than the fastest racing car. Sheku withdraws from her lips and stare straight into her eyes, she quickly lowers her pupils,

"I'm sorry, this is new to me".

"I know this is your first kiss, I'm sorry if I offended you Kumba, but I can't help it. You've been on my mind since the day I entered college;

I've been looking forward to going home every vacation to see your pretty face, but I guess you weren't as thrilled as I am". She felt guilty, if only he could see her heart and how much she cares.

"I don't—I mean-of course you know the rules, we're not allowed to date before the marriage ceremony, it's taboo" Kumba reminds him.

"This is the city Kumba, we're not in the village; here, when a boy likes a girl, they date for a while and get to know each other before marriage".

"But our parents don't believe in that Sheku, and if they find out we meet, my father will disown me and call off our wedding".

"No one will find out Kumba, I won't tell if you don't because I can't risk not being your future husband".

"I won't tell, I promise" she assures him,

"Then we'll act mature, wise and keep this between us", he embraced her again. "Are your Aunts and uncle treating you well?"

"Yes, I'm their oldest daughter and Aunty Josephine gives me everything, I don't need to ask".

"We'll be very careful, I'll think of a way we can meet and spend sometime together". "We have to go, Juliet will be worried" she got up in a hurry.

"Why the rush, your friend might not even be ready yet".

"You're a psychic now?"

"They were busy when we left".

"I need to get her, I have to get home or my

Aunts won't be happy".

"You're right, come on I'll tell Desmond to release her so you can leave, okay?" "Okay". He held her hand while walking towards the apartment building; once inside, Juliet was laying on Desmond's chest when they walked in.

"Where have you been Kumba, I thought you left, I was worried cause you don't know your way around" she sounds hysterical,

"Hello, you must be Juliet, I am Sheku, Desmond's roommate".

"Hello Sheku, I see you've met my friend Kumba already", she looks at their tightly held hands smiling. "My man Sheku, I see you've met Juliet's' best friend, she is the girl I had wanted you to meet, but I can see you like her huh, so we're out of the closet now?"

" I was never in the closet, this is the girl I was waiting for" Sheku happily told him.

"You mean you are not engaged to someone else?" he boldly asks.

"Yes I am engaged to her". Desmond and Juliet look at each other astounded.

"This is the girl Des" he calls Desmond for short,

"Kumba is my fiancé Des".

"Is she the one that you left in your village?"

"Yep, she's been here in the city for almost two years attending high school".

"Wow, this is great, did you girls plan this?"

"No Desmond, Kumba had told me of her

fiancé, but not his name and when we got here you didn't tell us your roommates' name did you?"

"You don't have to say another word Juliet. Desmond meet my fiancé Kumba" Sheku did the official introduction.

"Nice to meet you again Kumba" they all sat on the mat and laughed it off.

"Anyone hungry?" Desmond asks.

"I'm not, I have to get back or my Aunts will send a search party to look for me".

"Kumba is right, we have to go now" Juliet said, stands up and pulls Kumba with her. "We'll walk you" Sheku told them and follows.

"The poda-poda (the name for their local bus) will take long, I'll drive you ladies down", Desmond volunteers his service.

They sat in the front passenger seats, Kumba and Juliet sat in the back; Desmond was the only commentator in the ten or eleven years old car that smells of sweat. He chats all the way of his favorite soccer team 'The Eastend Lions', a team famous for having loud and bragging fans; rude and very violent towards their rival teams.

"When will I see you again?" Sheku quickly turned around and asked during one of Desmonds' pauses.

"My aunts don't let me go out, unless when I go to school and private tutoring" Kumba told him. She didn't understand why her aunts restrict her from visiting other friends; she's not even allowed to do grocery, they told her that's why they have maids. Uncle Sheik Abass provided his wives with two cooks, two maids for the children, two housecleaners and a gardener.

"I have to see you again Kumba".

"Set it up like me Kumba", Juliet intervened.

"We won't attend after school tutoring, we'll make up excuses with the teacher and make the trip up to the college".

"Listen, I drive too Kumba, I'll borrow Desmond's car to pick and drop you both off". How can she refuse his sweet puppy eyes?

"I can also pick you two up if Sheku is running late" Desmond wants to make sure they keep their dates.

CHAPTER 10

Everyone noticed the glow on Kumbas' face when she got home. "Another hundred on your term paper?" aunty Josephine asks cheerfully. Aunty Josephine always looks forward to receive Kumba's good grades and boasts to her high shot friends when they meet at the high table that sits only the rich businessmen's wives in the society. Secretly, Sheku and Kumba can't wait to meet at their hangout. Kumba had declined Juliet and Desmond's offer to pick them up; she has to be very careful and can't trust anyone; not when it comes to seeing a boyfriend. Juliet is a good friend, with loose tongue; it'll bring shame to her family and even cost her life if she slips her secret out. Few of her classmates' parents are in the same society group with her aunts. When a girl is suspected or known to have a boyfriend, the rumors spread like the wind. Mothers warn their daughters not to associate themselves with you and the community or society looks at you as a tramp.

Sheku saved up most of his salary to pay taxi fare once a week to pick up and drop off Kumba. He rented a room from an old Brazilian widow who was brought to Sierra Leone by her Sierra Leonean husband that passed away of cancer couple of years back. With her children all grown and gone, she refused to vacate the one land she fell in love with. Professor Campbell is her name and Sheku is her favorite student. Sheku insist to pay monthly for the little room at the back of her huge house they'd built closer away from the maids quarters for their favorite butler who passed away a year back. Mrs. Campbell can't grasp the fact that all cultures are different, especially Kumba's, where teenagers are forbidden to date openly. In Brazil where she came from, they're allowed to date freely, she'd narrate her story over an over again to Sheku of how she'd pursue her late husband and beg his closed heart to open up to hers. He'd ignored her, but she chases him until he accepts the fact she's the one for him. "I was treated like shit when he brought me home to meet the family" she smiled. "Listen child, if you love him, give your heart to him; my husband was forced to marry a second wife, but guess what child, my husband weighs my love for him and never left my side for her". Kumba will listen to one of her proud conquests. "You know what they say about us westerners, once we catch a man in bed, he never leaves"; she rolls her eyes with pride and smiles. In the tenth grade and going on fifteen, Kumba is aware of what takes place when a man and a woman are in bed. Single westerners are regarded as aggressive; it's believed that when they get hold of your man, it's less painful if you breakup with him right away. Westerners have a special magic potion that hunts the men they date and keeps them coming for more. Kumba had a western friend in the ninth grade and they shared lots of secrets, but there was one she didn't share, 'the magic potion'. The friend laughed when asked and told her it was a myth, and there's nothing called magic potion in their possession and if it's a potion, it's between their legs.

It's that day of the week again, its Saturday and she gets to spend almost the whole day with Sheku. Thanks to tutor Jones, who's a third year college student and tutors mathematics on weekends to make extra money, and also a friend of Sheku. He gets paid to teach Kumba on Saturdays and gets paid by Sheku for not complaining about the absence of his student. Kumba puts on her new print dress, she'd been to the saloon earlier and got her hair pressed and curled; she tries not to attract attention or get questioned about the fancy way she dressed. Kumba didn't rub her favorite bubble gum lip gloss that Sheku likes to lick off, she puts it in her bag and bid goodbye like the innocent simple good girl going for her tutoring.

"It's a full moon today, will you be home early to catch the fire flies and listen to Mammy Fatou's stories?" aunty Fatima asks her,

"Oh please, she don't need to rush home and listen to those witch stories, her studies are important", aunty Josephine defends her.

"I'll try not to be late, but you know how tutor Jones is, he likes to make sure I finish my work before he releases me".

"Don't say anymore my child, like I said, your school work is important, stay and finish your work". Kumba bid goodbye and runs off cause she hates it when her aunts fight to gain her affection. Kumba loves them, but aunty Fatima tends to be a little strict by implementing the village ways of raising a girl; with aunty Josephine being a city girl and with little education, she pretends to know more about raising a child even though she has none of her own; so Kumba gets away with everything. The couple of year's Kumba has been living with them, aunty Josephine has unofficially adopted her and insisted she calls her Mommy and aunty Fatima aunty.

Their hide out looks very different, Sheku was absent when Kumba opens the door with the spare key he gave her which makes it easier and doesn't have to wait restlessly outside for him or be forced to go into the big house and listen to

Hush Ma

Mrs. Campbell's love stories fear of being seen where she wasn't suppose to be. Kumba likes Mrs. Campbell, but sometimes gets bored by her long stories for she tells them over and over again. The shades were down, colorful candles lit instead of the kerosene lamp she's used to. The bed was neatly made, a bouquet of fresh red roses in a water vase was on each side of the bad and the sweet scent filled the air. Kumba turns on the television; pours some papaya juice and watch the local dancers introduce the new drum dance. Tired from the long ten-block walk, the nectar from the juice didn't help keep her pupils open; she slowly drifts off to sleep and dreamland. He was there, in her dream; she wasn't late, Sheku's hands were wide open to receive her. Kumba walked cheerfully into his big chest and felt his arms around her; his breath smells like chicken and vimto soft drink. "Hello my love, was I gone for a long time?" Reality hit her, she wasn't dreaming anymore, this is real; he was in the room, on the bed cuddling her in his masculine arms. Kumba opens her eyes to gaze into his warm eyes that has so many words to say,

"I miss you my love, do you miss me?" he brushes off the hair from her face, lips very close as he pins her beneath him before she can answer and their heartbeats is all you can hear. Kumba has made a promise never to fight him off, she loves him and looks forward to bear his name in holy matrimony and be the mother of his children. He runs his tongue around her lips sending chills and goose bumps all over her tiny frame; his sweet breath clouds her face as she closes her eyes to avoid contact with his.

"Are you still shy?" Sheku teasingly pokes her ribs and enjoys watching her twitch. "Mm-mm-m-em" she mumbles and swallows the gulp of saliva in her throat. Sheku parts her lips and gets hold of her tongue. Kumba enjoys the rolling of their tongues in the slimy warmth of their mouths; he slowly pulls away and sucks at the nape of her neck as his big hands pulls up her skirt and softly caresses her thighs. It feels like millions of needles piercing her virgin skin that was rubbed down with goat milk and shea butter. She is confused of the signals her stomach was sending her brain or is she having diarrhea or just nerves of extreme excitement. Kumbas' heart beats faster to every touch of his soft hands and suddenly the room gets hotter, the fan was no help; she dug her fingers into the hay mattress to get control of her trembling body.

"Just relax honey, I promise, I won't hurt you". Her mind went back to the horrible stories her friends had shared around of their first time with a guy; this is different, she knows cause she's in love with Sheku and it's also taboo to sleep or make love to a man out of wedlock. Sheku's going to be her husband, the thought scares her of regretting whatever will happen. Girls are aware that if you give it up before the wedding night, the man will consider you cheap and don't marry you, the worst part is, decent men don't want left over, so you're stuck being a mistress. Will she be considered a left over if she gives up her virginity before marriage?

"No, no Sheku, I can't do this, it's wrong, you know it", she wiggles from underneath him.

"Will you relax, I'm not other guys, I'll still marry you regardless of what we do here today". Kumba looks away with shame for not trusting him.

"Kumba, I won't do anything you don't want me to, I love you, it's hard to be closer and don't touch you" he gently caressed the side of her cheekbone.

"Come, sit up and see the food that I brought" he changes the intimate and intense subject to food.

"Can I guess?" she asks,

"Oh come on, you already know, you can smell it" Sheku has been very attentive; he knows what she wants and will get it to please her. He gets up to show her the food and she notices her half naked body; she jumps up and quickly pulls down her skirt in shame. "Oh come on, take it off and relax, it'll all be mine soon anyway" he pinch her butt and she jumps higher and screeches.

"Come here" he pulls her tiny frame into his broad chest,

"You're not going to be one of those wives that do everything in the dark, right?" he asks and kisses her forehead.

"What do you mean?"

" You're not going to only want to make love in the dark and hide this beautiful body from me right?" he lift her chin to gaze into her big lovely eyes.

"Why do you want to see me naked, that's wrong"? She protests for her dignity. "No Kumba, it's not wrong, we're in the twenty first century, and things change; you're an intelligent girl and very smart, let's not behave like our ancestors before us, lets love each other openly and explore what had never been done". She was out of touch and has no clue where this is leading.

"Kumba, when I marry you, you'll be my one and only wife, I promise not to ever share you if you promise to give me your heart". Kumba pinched herself hoping it's a dream and it's time to wake up, she wasn't dreaming, it's reality.

"You won't be marrying two or three wives?" she hesitantly asks,

"I don't need two or three wives when I have one that's worth more than three. And why should I marry so many wives, it's not right, there's no where in the Quran that states a man has to marry more than one wife".

"It's our culture Sheku, your family will not allow it".

"Kumba, I am not putting any woman of mine through what my mother was forced to accept because she had no choice. I want my wife to have a choice not to share me with another woman, and also I want to be at peace that I love only one woman, not to be a hypocrite".

"Why do you talk like that Sheku, your father is an Imam with more than five wives, he'll cast you out if you refuse to marry a member of his mosque's daughter," she reminds him.

"Kumba, listen, I have a plan, promise me you won't tell anyone".

"I promise" she agrees excitedly that he can share secrets with her.

"When I graduate next year, I'm leaving".

"Leaving, to where?" "I am working with the dean of my college who's helping to get me a scholarship so that I can further my studies in America",

"America, now I know why you don't want to marry more than one wife, you're getting westernized"

"Kumba, I'm not condemning our culture; I like it, but it's not for me".

"This is how you plan your life, date me, leave for America to marry a westerner and never come back, huh?" she angrily pushed him off.

"No, you can't just shrug me like that, you're going about this wrongly. I love you Kumba, when I get to America, I'll get a job while I'm studying so that I can purchase your ticket to join me".

"You mean I'm going to America too" she happily grins.

"Of course, you're going to be my wife, and

as my wife, I'll need you by my side", Sheku plants another kiss on her lips. Kumba wraps her arms around his neck and returns the kiss. It's a long thirty seconds kiss that leaves them both breathless and shaking. Sheku swaps her off to the bed without any resistance and carefully lays her tiny frame on the bed; slowly, he unbuttons her blouse and unveils her donut breasts. Kumba didn't flinch, she let him take charge and lay still as he pulls her skirt off leaving the slender legs bare.

"You're so beautiful Kumba, I'll always cherish your body" she giggles like the schoolgirl she is to his compliment. Sheku stands up and starts taking off his shirt and pant. Kumba's heart skips a beat as she fights to control her nerves taking deep breaths and closing her eyes for a second. When she opens them, he was naked at the foot of the bed. Kumba had seen a naked baby boy, but not a naked grown boy; his penis is bigger and erect, and his chest hairy. Sheku crawls between her legs pulls off her panties and tossed them on the floor. Her whole body is trembling out of control; Sheku rolls over by her side and cuddles her naked body in his.

"Remember what I told you, I will never hurt you Kumba, I just need to know that you trust me".

"I do trust you, but I'm scared" she reminds him.

" I know my love, come, I'll take the fear away",

he pulls her closer to him and sings softly a tribal song that his forefathers sang to a woman they love. The sweet lullaby is soothing and sends her off to sleep; sheku pulls the sheet over their bodies and joins her in dreamland.

CHAPTER 11

LIKE THE SAYING, "YOU hear with one ear and pass it out the other" was her days at school. Kumba's mind was focused on that one afternoon with Sheku; they've shared so much that helps their love grow more. She didn't share her new encounter with her friends; she kept it buried inside safe and sound. Everyone asks her why she's so extra happy, but aunty Josephine shuns them off and calls them witches who hate to see other people happy. Sheku had really made a way for their love to grow, shows her things she'd never dreamt would touch her in unbelievable places but still protect her honor by making sure she remains a virgin until the womanhood society proclaims she's a woman and ready to face the next step of her life which will be getting married, bear his children and be a good house wife.

As the months drew near for Sheku's departure, Kumba finds it very difficult. She has become attached to him; with two years left of her high school, she succumbs to insomnia. A week before his departure to America, Sheku's parents made it official; they visited Kumba's father, Chief Pa Sorie, to pay the dowry on their son's behalf. A letter was delivered to her uncle and aunts for them to be aware that Sheku's now engaged to her. Part of her dowry money was sent to uncle Sheik Abass as a gift for the role he played in helping to raise her. In the letter, Chief Pa Sorie instructs his brother to keep Kumba in his house until Sheku finished his studies in America and sends for her.

Three days before his departure to the United States, Sheku and Kumba found a hide away hotel by the beach and they decide to spend the day together, away from all the distractions. "I am going to miss you terribly" was his first words as they got to the hotel. "You'll write and call, won't you?"

"Of course, my body will be in America, but my mind and soul will be here with you, my love" he pulls her closer, kisses her big and succulent lips moisturized by sweet strawberry fruit. Kumba pulls away forty seconds into the intense kiss and slowly unbuttons the new dress she got as a gift from her in-laws.

"Wow, are we in a hurry to go somewhere?" he

hesitantly asks.

"Yes, I'm going somewhere with you. Sheku, let's take our love somewhere. Somewhere we've never been before, to the next level, I am more than ready".

"Kumba, what are you saying?"

"What I'm saying is, I need you Sheku, I can't wait no more Sheku, I am seventeen going on eighteen, if we were in the village, I would have been married with four or five kids. But look at me Sheku, an old maid, all my friends are with family and I am still a virgin", she peacefully protested.

"Kumba, I thought we agreed on waiting".

"For what Sheku, I am your fiancé".

"Yes, but there are steps and a culture we have to follow until we become husband and wife".

"Oh, there you go again with the culture thing. I thought everything that people believe is a myth, what's the change of mind?"

"There's no change of mind Kumba, we have to give your family their respect, let the old folks initiate you into the womanhood society, and when you're a woman, we can take our love to the next level" he reminds her.

"Making love now, or after the womanhood initiations makes no difference to me".

"I am in no position to bring shame on your family. Those old folks can talk, especially if they found you not to be a virgin before marriage". Kumba takes a deep breath and throws her naked body on the bed.

"Are you mad?"

"No I am not, just a little disappointed, but I'll be your wife soon and we'll make love one day".

"That's my girl. I love you, come here, we can still foreplay right?" Kumba look forward to his caress, kisses and his soft tongue that licks her in forbidden places that makes her scream for more.

Sheku has an early flight. Uncle Sheik Abass had forbidden her from taking off school to escort him to the airport. Sheku called her early before she left for school to say goodbye and promised to write and call frequently. It was tough on her the first month of his absence; she focused on the good times they spent together to help get her on. Sheku writes once a month and calls bi-weekly to hear Kumba's voice. Kumba's last year of high school was really hectic; her studies had given her no time to reply to Sheku's mail and she hoped he understands how stressful final year can be. Kumba passed all her subjects and was accepted with scholarship to the number one college in Freetown. Kumba hadn't spend the past two summer vacations with her parents in the village, she decided to spend the last summer vacation of her high school with them before heading off to college. Kumba planned to study nursing. Sheku who graduated pre-med in the same college she's been accepted left her most of his science books.

Mama Siah looks like her older sister instead of her mother. Chief Pa Sorie is very proud of his daughter and shows her off to his friends in the village. Kumba is one of them, not an educated city girl; she works on Mama Siah's farm and cooks for the household.

Kumba's life changed when she was kidnapped in the middle of the night by the female elders of the village and carried into the woods. She'd heard stories of such kidnappers. She willingly follows their instructions, blind- folded with one of her mother's head ties, she waits anxiously and curious about what will be her fate. She was naked and can hear female voices all around her surroundings.

"Come on Chief Papa Sorie's princess, we're making you into a woman today", an old feeble voice told her. Kumba is told to lie down, blindly; she touches around to feel for the bed.

"What are you looking for, there's no bed my child, you have to lie on the floor" the voice instructs her. Kumba holds on tight to the only support she has, which was a hand holding hers, then uses her knees to support her frail body to the cold wet floor. Lying on her back, she feels someone sit on her chest with her arms pinned down, legs spread apart with people sitting on them. She tries to wiggle but was unable. The kidnappers are too strong. The weight on her chest was heavy which makes her short of breath; Kumba tried to relax feared she'll stop breathing and die, she decided to call onto the one thing that'll help. "God, I am weak and tired of fighting these people. Please help me relax and take whatever they're going to do to me" she fainted. A severe burning feeling woke her up hours later, someone had poured a bottle of rubbing alcohol on her vagina and it stings and was painful. The blindfold is off, she stares around and sees other girls on the floor naked like her; their only covering is a piece of cloth folded three or four times like a sanitary pad placed neatly between their legs. Kumba didn't know why she has such excruciating pain between her legs. The urge to use the bathroom has been taunting her but she was too scared to go and afraid she couldn't hold it no more. The elders help carry her into the washroom and left. Kumba slowly removes the cloth between her legs, there was freshly grounded leaves covered with blood. Was it her period? No, it was more than that. Something was done when she'd passed out. Kumba's friends at school were not spreading rumors; her clitoris had been cut off or circumcised when she fainted. Urinating makes the situation worst, it stings and hurts, she screams through out the long process. The elders were chanting and dancing happily, their reason, Kumba is now a woman. Leaving the washroom, she walks by an open door and witnesses the drastic scene. There is a girl on the floor naked; four women, one sitting on her chest, one on either legs pulling them apart, the fourth woman was kneeling between her legs with a little knife cutting away what seems to be the girl's virgin clitoris. Kumba watches closely, the lady held on to the upper end of the vulva skin or clitoris, which is the biological name. She first uses the knife to draw a line on both sides, then holding them together, starts at the apex of the now bleeding tissue and slowly slices it off from its attachment. There was no noise because the girl's mouth was stuffed with cloth, but she was alert because she wriggles hard to every slicing. Speechless, and frozen, she now figures out what was done to her. One of the ladies notices Kumba and shuts the door in her face then yells for escorts who came and carry her back to her room.

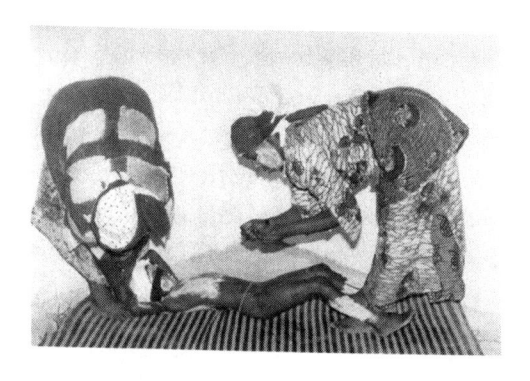

The healing process was slow but the scar remains not only between her legs, but also in her mind of that dreadful day. Back in the city and her first year in college, Kumba couldn't concentrate. The memories hunt her every move that made her fail first semester and didn't reply to her fiancée's letters.

Sheku finished second year of medical school and decided to make the trip home on school vacation to marry his fiancée. He was happy when his parents wrote to inform him that Kumba was now a woman and to hurry back to make her his wife, but was tormented throughout his twelve hours flight home over why his fiancée never replied to his recent mails. She always has excuses not to pick up his calls; he was told she is sleeping, studying or she went for her private tutoring was all he's been told for the past four months and was about to find out the truth. At the airport, Kumba was no show. Aunty Josephine assured him everything was fine and it'll be better if they stay apart until the wedding day. Sheku had arrived a week before their wedding and puts up by his uncle who also lodged his parents and extended family members in the huge mansion his rich uncle had built since he found new wealth in diamonds. The wedding separation was boring for him. Sheku's focus was Kumba; he hadn't seen her in two years and the sudden change in the past months kept him baffled about where their love is heading.

Aunty Josephine had got all the exfoliating recipes from her friends and prepared each one of them. Kumba didn't care about all the excitement of the wedding both families had agreed to have in the city. Chief Pa Sorie hired five buses to transport the families and friends he'd invited to the almost celebrity event. It's a big deal in Sierra Leone or a third world country when your daughter's fiancé is coming from America, a first world, to wed her. Aunty Josephine hired all the local drummers and dancers; there was food everywhere, and even though Chief Pa Sorie was against alcohol, he went the extra mile to order some for his drinking friends and gave the okay to his neighboring tribal Locko Chief to bring gallons of palm wine to the ceremony.

Kumba was been kept confined at the head godmother's house with a daily hectic schedule. Her godmothers, Mama Siah and aunty Josephine wake her up at four thirty in the morning for the ritual bath. From head to toes, she's washed down with herbs and fruits; her slender figure is waxed with different beauty recipes aunty Josephine had gathered. Kumba wasn't allowed to do anything; she's given a potion that makes her sleep. The old folks believe that a well-rested bride to be will have enough energy on her wedding night. Her last night as a virgin; the women that had kidnapped her for the womanhood ceremonies were in the room with the godmothers for that special talk. "Kumba my child, you're going into the second phase of womanhood," one of the old folks told her.

"Tomorrow is a special day, but the best part will be the honeymoon, we want to prepare you for the first night of marriage, it's a very special night; your family is counting on you to make them proud". Kumba knows what to expect, her friends and biology classes were a bit of help. But until that first night, she didn't know how she'd feel when it's all over.

"Are you ready my child?" her mind drifted off during the old woman's speech. "Yes Ma, I'm ready" Kumba played it off.

"You will respect your husband, you should never talk when he talks, you'll allow him to punish you if you're bad, you'll cook his meals, you'll bear his children and never, never object to him taking another wife. Are you ready for your duty to be a wife?"

"Yes madam" her fatigued mouth responded.

"Hip, hip, hip" her godmother yells,

"Hooray!" all the ladies responded.

"Do we have a bride here?" she asks,

"Yes we do" they responded.

"Is she a happy bride?" her godmother asked again.

"Yes she is" they responded,

"Hip, hip, hip"

"Hooray," they all chanted as Kumba drifted of to sleep by the potion.

The big day was here, Kumba was bathed early, and her waxed skin was rubbed down with shea butter. The hairdresser was the first to come in and style her hair; the makeup lady was next, then the godmother to don her in the wedding gown she bought in Paris. All dressed up, she was allowed to take a quick glance at herself, maybe it was the mirror exaggerating because Kumba couldn't believe how pretty she looked. The veil was use to cover her face, as she was led into the Mercedes Benz waiting outside. Everyone was at the mosque waiting anxiously. The godmothers who protect her from the well-wishers lead in Kumba. Sheku is in place with his godfathers on either side of him. He'd change a lot in two years, his complexion was a little lighter, smooth skin and he'd grown a mustache. Unfortunately, the veil couldn't allow Sheku to see her beautiful face; they faced the Imam as he read from the holy Quran the reason to get married, the rules of being a good husband or a good wife. Sheku had a sleepless night thinking of this special day, he'd tried many times to speak with Kumba, but was forbidden by his godfathers. Before his departure to the United States, he'd left behind a happy fiancée, Kumba has changed since she was pronounced a woman; with her strange behavior, Sheku was left to guess what went wrong. It can't be another guy cause gossipers would've alarmed him, but on the other hand, Kumba is very secretive. Sheku's been faithful to her for two years, he's scared the wedding might be a mistake; she is the same girl that begged for his love. When asked to kiss the bride, Sheku quickly lifts up the veil to see the angelic face he'd missed. Their eyes locked into each other as they shared the kiss.

"Hello my beautiful bride" is the first sentence

that comes out after the kiss. She is speechless and refuses to take her eyes off him,

"I miss you my love, look at you, and you've grown so much" Kumba smiles,

" Did you miss me?"

"Yes, yes—I'm happy to see you—I'm—I mean you have a mustache".

"You like it, if you don't, I'll take it off".

"No don't, I like it, you've changed a lot yourself".

"It's the new environment, the weather in America usually has an effect on everyone; come on, we'll talk about us later, let's thank the organizers and well-wishers". Sheku takes her hand as they make it through the crowds thanking everyone for coming to their special day. The wedding reception was the talk of the town, because both fathers of the newly weds are chiefs. The president of the country was invited to introduce them. There were plenty of tribal foods to feed a whole country, lots of drinks, different tribe drummers competing to be the cheering crowds' favorite. At twelve midnight, the Godparents snuck them away from the crowd to a cabin by the beach Sheku had rented for their honeymoon. Alone at last, Kumba went into the bathroom and locked herself. She took off the elegant evening gown, shoes, and jumps under the shower to wash off the sweat and makeup. The knock on the door startled her,

"Kumba, are you okay?"

"Yes, I'm almost finished" she answered him. Kumba covers up when she exits the bathroom and it baffles Sheku who was expecting his bride to come out naked and run into his waiting arms. Without a word, he makes his way into the bathroom to wash off his sweat. Kumba was under the sheets covered from head to toe. Sheku figures they had a long day and it'll be better if he let her rest, he silently sneaks under the covers.

"You're back" she turns around to face him.

"Yes, hush, go to sleep you had a long and tiring day".

"It's our honeymoon, we shouldn't be sleeping".

"I know my love, we have the rest of our lives together, come here, let's rest, we'll do all our talking tomorrow" he pulls her into his big chest and wraps his arms around her as she drifts off to sleep.

The smell of boiled cassava and fried fish stew fills her nostrils as she wakes up. Sheku's been up, showered and dressed. Kumba is embarrassed to be left in bed; she'd already broke the first rule,

"Never allow your husband to get out of bed before you, that'll make you a lazy house wife". She bows her head in shame,

"Kumba, don't be embarrassed, if it'll make you better, listen, I had to get up early to call my friends in America; I had promised to let them know how the wedding turned out". He pulls off the covers from her,

"Come, I'll help you into the shower".

"Thanks, I can do it myself" Kumba sprung off the bed, into the bathroom and quickly shuts the door behind her. Sheku went to get some sodas. When he returns, Kumba is dressed and eating.

"Where were you, I'm almost finishing the food".

"I went to get more drinks. Eat up, I had some food earlier and am still full",

"Good, more for me",

"Eat up, you need to have some flesh on them bones", she looks up at him and he was scared he'd said the wrong words.

"Am I too bony for you?"

"No, no, I don't, I mean, am sorry, the words came out wrong".

" It's okay, what I need is some of your American vitamins".

"How much do you weigh?" Sheku picks his words carefully.

"I guess about one hundred and ten or fifteen pounds".

"You're the same weight since I left, you've grown taller though, I like that".

"That's all you like?"

"Come here let's talk, we have a lot to catch up on", Kumba bravely joins him on the bed.

"Why did you sleep in these last night?" he tugs on the nightgown,

"I was cold" she lied. "Look at me Kumba, you've been acting very strange, have I done something wrong, where's our love baby, is there someone else?" the questions rambled out,

"No Sheku, there's no one else, I love you, but things change" she paused.

"Something happened". Sheku's mind wanders off and waits impatiently for the bad news.

"Kumba, you're my wife now, it doesn't mater how bad it is, I'll never stop loving you" he assures her.

"They hurt me Sheku, they really hurt me", she burst out crying.

"Who hurt you Kumba? You can tell me baby, it'll be okay" he pulls her closer and wipes off her tears.

"The ladies at the womanhood society hurt me Sheku, they took something precious away from me," she sobs uncontrollably. Sheku is relieved, he's now aware why Kumba was behaving strangely.

"But honey, I thought you knew this will happen?"

"What, to be circumcised?"

"Sh-hh, be careful, the walls can hear you, I thought you're not supposed to talk about it".

"It's wrong Sheku, I heard rumors of what takes place when a girl gets initiated into the womanhood society, but I never believe it because other tribes don't practice it".

"It's partially my fault Kumba, we're open with each other, I should've told you what to expect when you got initiated", Sheku tries to console her.

"I have no more sexual feelings Sheku, am scared I'll only be like a dead corpse in bed with you, not able to please you".

"Don't worry Kumba, I love you regardless; our grandmothers, mothers went through the same procedure and can still fulfill their husbands needs; our love will help us get through it" he gently placed a kiss on her wet lips and wiped off the tears that run down her cheeks. Kumba wraps her arms around Sheku's neck and pulls him down for a real kiss. No words were exchanged during the foreplay, he was right; every stroke of his hand on her bare skin sends chills and goose bumps all over the tiny frame waiting to receive her knight in shiny Armour. Kumba utters one scream of joy when he took her virginity; they cry together and console each other. The elders were happy; they get the sheet with blood that proves their little princess was a flower that had been deflowered.

It was hard to say goodbye to her families and friends, she's now married and starting a new life with Sheku. America is what she'd dreamt of; with the help of Sheku in her new environment, Kumba enrolls in nursing school. Ten years later, a registered nurse married to a successful doctor and a mother of three adorable children, two girls and a boy; Kumba makes frequent trips to her homeland where she'd set up a clinic. Kumba recruits trained nurses to reach out to girls and women in the different tribal communities, encourages them to have a higher education, stop being a man's second or third wife and fight to ban female genital mutilations.

At her second home in America, Kumba works at a Planned Parenthood clinic that provides services to unwed teenagers and abused women. Her shift ends at three p.m. With the last patient out the door, Kumba rushes home to catch her favorite show, 'The Oprah Winfrey show'. On this particular day, the hard working nurse has to stop by a sick patient's house to drop off his medications. It's not her job description, but Kumba will go to the end of the earth to help. She missed forty minutes of her favorite show. Sitting on the couch in the haven she calls home surrounded by her children, Kumba got to hear her role model, her favorite talk show host Oprah and her hero tell women in America how lucky they are to be born and raised in the blessed land called America. Kumba's been raising her two daughters to have a mind of their own, to marry who they love, never to share their man with another woman and keep what it takes to please their man. They are lucky to be born in America, she's guaranteed her daughters won't have to face the female genital mutilation that's forced on girls in her hometown by ignorant cultural beliefs that left a scar in her mind. With each of her precious daughters tucked under her hands watching the show, Kumba held them tight, closed her eyes and talk to God. "God, there's nothing better I can ask for. I thank you for the strength you've installed in me. God, I know you made women out of love, but I am still confused why we go through so many obstacles in life. I have faith in you God; you're a miracle God and would help every woman in this world to overcome all negative obstacles in their lives. And God please bless our fathers, brothers, uncles and sons to better understand and respect all women in their lives. Amen.

THE END!

ABOUT THE AUTHOR

Mamet is a freelance writer residing in Pennsylvania with her family.

Writing has been a hobby since the age of ten.

Mamet wants her readers not to only enjoy her books, but also be aware of what's going on around the world. Look for Mamet's other books coming out soon:

MAMET'S OTHER BOOKS

STRIKER

Other people's information, credit cards, checks, and counterfeit money have given Melissa a luxurious life. At the peak of her success which causes pain and suffering to her victims, Mel fell in love with a man of the law and is forced to give up her income source. Mel is torn between two worlds with a tough choice to make.

KEEP THE MAN; I'LL KEEP THE RING

For fifteen years, Kelly gave her heart, soul and body to David. In return he can only guaranty his heart to her. David learned that he has an incurable cancer and is struck with the bad news that he only has three months to live. Can David break his marriage and give his body and soul to Kelly in time?

Printed in the United Kingdom
by Lightning Source UK Ltd.
130372UK00001B/10/P